BORN FIGHTER

BORN
FIGHTER

Reg Kray

ARROW

First published in Arrow 1991

9 11 13 15 17 19 20 18 16 14 12 10

First published in the United Kingdom in 1990 by Century
Random House, 20 Vauxhall Bridge Road, London SW1V 2SA

Arrow Books Limited
Random House UK Ltd, 20 Vauxhall Bridge Road, London SW1V 2SA

Random House Australia (Pty) Limited
20 Alfred Street, Milsons Point, Sydney,
New South Wales 2061, Australia

Random House New Zealand Limited
18 Poland Road, Glenfield
Auckland 10, New Zealand

Random House South Africa (Pty) Limited
PO Box 337, Bergvlei, South Africa

Random House UK Limited Reg. No. 954009

A CIP catalogue record for this book
is available from the British Library

Papers used by Random House UK Limited
are natural, recyclable products made from wood grown in
sustainable forests. The manufacturing processes conform to
the environmental regulations of the country of origin.

ISBN 0 09 987810 0

Printed and bound in Great Britain by
Cox & Wyman Ltd, Reading, Berkshire

DEDICATION

I dedicate this book to my late parents. On behalf of Ron and myself, I would like to thank them for everything they have given us in life. Yesterday, today and tomorrow belong to them, and all three they gave to us. We have, in the past, shared sorrow and joy with our parents, but, in their presence, there has always been more joy than sorrow. They taught us not to be cynical about love. For—to quote from *Desiderata*—'in the face of all aridity and disenchantment, love is perennial as the grass, and with all its sham, drudgery and broken dreams, it is still a beautiful world.'

ACKNOWLEDGEMENTS

Many thanks to Ron Kray, Peter Gillett, Carol Clerk, Stephen Gold and Mark Booth for helping to make this book possible.

Reg Kray

CONTENTS

FOREWORD

A long time ago, I felt like I had a dam within me which was ready to burst: I wanted to tell the life story of Ron and me. We began work with Fred Dinenage on the book *Our Story*, which was published in 1988. However, the manuscript passed through various hands and, by the time *Our Story* reached the shops, it contained many errors and distortions. It was like the *Beano* comic with Alf Garnett dialogue.

One Sunday, shortly afterwards, in September of that year, I switched on the radio early and heard *Thought for the Day* by the Rabbi Hugo Gryn. He said that sometimes when one aims at a target with a bow, one may miss because of bad vision, a distraction or not having enough strength to pull the bow. He went on to say that, according to God, one should aim again.

I took courage from this talk. I am never satisfied with half measures in anything I do, and so I decided to aim the bow again until the arrow could reach the target of truth. *Born Fighter* is the true account of my life with Ron and, as much as I have enjoyed the telling, I feel confident that the story of the Kray twins has only just begun.

INTRODUCTION

A STEP TOWARDS FREEDOM

Wednesday 19 April 1989 was the day I had waited twenty-one years for. It was the day I left the dispersal system for good and set off for Lewes, a Category B prison near Brighton.

I woke early, before 3 am, on my last morning at HMP Gartree, Leicestershire, and had a cup of tea from my flask. I thought of the night before, when I had said the last goodbyes to my friends Mick Bartley and Mick Archer. We had shared adversity and laughs together for two years, but now we had to part, each of us to go our separate ways, but in the hope we would eventually meet again in better circumstances and surroundings.

I left Gartree Prison at 10.30 am and, after a changeover stop an hour later, got on to a large coach to go to Wormwood Scrubs for a few nights. There were fifteen of us. I was beside a young feller called Warren Davey. We were cuffed in the new way, his right hand to my right hand, which made our movement more difficult. Warren stood out against the rest; he was so polite, clean and tidy in dress and, although he was doing six years, he seemed entirely out of place in prison.

We got to the Scrubs at about 5 pm. We had a meal and a cup of tea, checked our gear, and then went to the storeroom for clothes. A con who works in the stores asked me for my autograph, which I gave him. We then came on to D-Wing to be allocated cells, and I could hear voices calling me from upstairs on the "3" landing. It was my old friends Alf Barkley, Ray Johnson and others. They came down, gave me tea bags and milk and generally helped Warren and me to settle in. A few cons I didn't know came to shake hands with me, and so did others I had met over the years.

There was an old, tall tree right outside my cell window, full of white flowers. It was beautiful.

Earlier on, in reception, I saw a large cardboard box with the words "Kray back record" on it. I must have one of the largest record sheets there is. I first came to the Scrubs at sixteen years of age when Ron and I were remanded on a charge of grievous bodily harm on the police and we did another month there when we were eighteen for assault on the police. I had been back just three years ago in the chokey block (segregation or punishment unit) for a month, and now I was back again. One could get to like that place! The Scrubs does have a good atmosphere.

They all asked how Ron was and sent their best wishes, and I was pleased to be back in London for a week. It's still the best city in the world, still a great city of glamour. As I came through the concrete jungle in the coach, I felt exhilarated. The streets looked beautiful.

All through that week, my friends there really went out of their way to make Warren and me welcome. People were coming to my cell to shake hands or to tell their different stories, and this made me feel touched and very humble. One young coloured kid who had just got a life sentence came to my cell to seek my advice on how to get through his time, and also asked me to sign a photo to his parents. Warren and I made the kid a cup of tea and I gave him advice in the hope it will help him.

Even the screws there think I should be out. At least three of them stopped me on the landing and said so.

I left the Scrubs at 11 am on Tuesday 25 April in a coach full of young people, who were nice and lively. Again, I was handcuffed to my friend Warren. It's the first time I've ever been in a coach with a TV in it.

It was really smashing going through London for the second time in a week. I saw all the old names and signs which I had not seen for twenty-one years—Charringtons beer advertising from pub signs, Joe Coral's betting shops. Though I was the oldest in the coach, I did not feel older than the rest. It was as though I had not aged, and also as though I had never been away from London, although I saw the new phone boxes in place of the old red booths and I also noticed the new type of compact toilets that looked like something out of space.

The humour in the coach coming from all the young prisoners was really special. One kid, Carl, looked out of the coach window and saw a helicopter. He said, "Look, there's a helicopter on the way to Gartree!" Carl and I had been at Gartree when the helicopter escape took place.

Then, as the screw was taking the handcuffs off a black kid and a white kid when we arrived at the change-over point at Feltham, one of the young fellers said, "The time of blacks being in chains is over!" And again we all laughed aloud. I felt really good to be with people who were so happy, even though they faced part of their future in adversity. I will never forget them. They were a smashing bunch.

When we entered the building at Feltham, we all had to go to different rooms, like large cells, and I shook hands with Warren, who was going to a different prison.

I was the last one to leave, in a coach of my own. It drove over a flyover, and I remembered the stupid stories of how I was supposed to have buried somebody beneath one. We travelled on and the ride was beautiful. I could see the light at the end of the tunnel to eventual freedom. I could already smell the crisp sea air from Lewes Downs . . .

CHAPTER 1

IN THE BEGINNING

Sometimes when the wind is howling outside my cell, I lie back in my bed with the radio on, hardly listening. My thoughts are miles away in the past. The faces of yesterday come alive to my eyes and I wonder where some of my old friends have gone, and what they are doing now. I think of how much I would like to have a chat with them, but, alas, it is not to be. Time and distance can be so sad.

On Sundays, the hymns on Radio Two remind me of Wormwood Scrubs, when Ron and I were sixteen years of age in the prison church with all the young offenders. I can still see all their faces.

Time has taken many of our old friends from us, through death, and we are left with just the memories . . . and the dreams.

Recently, I dreamed I was twenty-three again. I was in the Regent Canal dock area of London with my late friend Billy Jones. I woke up, and as I lay in the darkness with my thoughts, I could see the faces before me—Billy Jones, Jim Harris, Reg Olds, all friends who are no longer with us. They will not be at the gate to meet me when I get out, but I know they will be there in spirit.

My main regret in life is that I wasn't in the company of my parents for long enough. I suppose, like us all, I now realize I took them too much for granted and thought they would be with us forever.

Not long ago, I dreamed I was once again in the company of my mother and my Uncle Jack. I suddenly woke to the familiar surroundings of my cell, to my great disappointment and sorrow. Twenty-two years in prison and I still get flashbacks to the past, to other times and other places which I have enjoyed. It must be some sort of safety valve that works in my sleep to induce good feelings.

The memories I most cherish of my late parents are from the days when we all lived together at 178 Vallance Road, Bethnal Green, in the East End of London. We had moved there at an early age from Stene Street, Hoxton, less than a mile away, where Ron and I were born on 24 October 1933.

Number 178 was a lucky old house. It had a big oak door with a large knocker, and the people used to call it "Fort Vallance", a name which was given to it by a feller called the "Curly King". It was a terraced house with a toilet out in the yard. Ron and I used to love the kitchen. We had a big coal fire, and we used to sit around it while our mother used to be doing the ironing or making pots of stew or cups of tea.

When we were kids, Ron and I used to sleep in the back room, and sometimes we would lie there in the mornings listening to my mother, Violet, singing Vera Lynn songs. She had a melodious singing voice with good resonance and as I listened, I used to get great comfort and a feeling of belonging, as though we were in our own mansion and not just a terraced house.

My old man, as we referred to my father Charles, was a man of few words, but he had a good personality and when I would walk into the small kitchen, he would proudly say to me: "Your mother has a good voice, hasn't she? She should've been a singer." And I would nod in agreement while he poured me a cup of tea.

He used to keep chickens in the back yard, which we would eventually eat. I remember once a little chick, just a few days old, fell into a bowl of water, and appeared to be dead. My old man placed it on a cloth in the oven with the gas on warm, and the bird recovered. Afterwards, it used to follow my father all over the kitchen.

The old man always used to have parties in the house, and my mother was always a good hostess. Never once did my parents turn away anyone who had nowhere to sleep or was in need of a meal. All our friends would be welcome, even if they were wanted by the law. I suppose that's why I've always liked plenty of company, and this has helped me in prison, because I'm used to waking up with people around me.

Despite what has been written about us in the past, it's not true that Ron ever struck the old man, although there used to be many arguments, just like most families in the East End had in those days. My old man was on the run from the army for twelve years, so he had some excuse to turn to drink, seeing that his family life had been so disrupted, but I never forgot that he went on the run in the first place to look after us when we were young. I have always been proud of him. It was he who first took Ron and me to the Robert Browning youth club in South London for boxing lessons. He would take us on a number 8 bus from Bethnal Green to Camberwell three times a week to train at the club.

He was always immaculate in dress, and would go to the barber's every day for a shave. He would also have a bet each day, and his regular haunt for drinking would be the "99" public house in Liverpool Street.

From an early age, Ron and I would both go to the same barber shop, just round the corner from Vallance Road. It was called "Ben the Barber's" by everyone in the neighbourhood. Ben was a medium-sized Jewish feller who had jet-black hair, pushed right back in the 1920s style. He had a young assistant by the name of Raymond. People would sit patiently on the chairs that were placed at the back of the shop, reading all the magazines and newspapers while they waited for Ben to call out, "Next, please". Opposite the chairs where the customers sat for haircuts and shaves were notices advertising things for sale—Gillette blades, Brylcrèem and Durex. In those days, Durex were five a packet for two shillings and sixpence. I used to watch as Ben would quietly slip a packet into a customer's hand as though it were some big secret.

Each Saturday the Relay radio—everyone used to hire radios in those days—would blare out the football figures and results. Most of the customers were either Arsenal or Spurs supporters. The door of the little shop would be wide open, and all the neighbours, people like Mr McDougal, Mr Morten and Mr Miller, would call in "Hello, Ben" as they passed by. Ben would please Ron and me by saying how quiet and still we'd been sitting in the chair during the haircut, and we would tell this proudly to our mother when we returned home.

After our short back and sides, Ron and I would tip Ben either a sixpence or a shilling, and then go off to our little house up Vallance Road. Just as we would leave Ben's shop, we'd see Mr and Mrs George Gillett sitting at the doorstep of their house, just at the side of the barber's, having their tea and a chat. Mrs Gillett would sit on a wooden chair at the side of the street door which would be held wide open by a large round grey stone placed at its base. The Gilletts had had this stone for years. They were both very tall and broad in build. They had thick grey hair. Mr Gillett was always in shirt sleeves, with his thick trouser braces showing. The kids nearby would be playing on the cobblestone road, yelling and shouting. They had a game called "Touch", and another called "Release". Others would be playing football or cricket with a tennis ball.

In those days, even the weather seemed better. The sun always seemed to be shining. I can remember my favourite clothes being a grey pair of flannels, a white shirt and a pair of plimsolls that had been brightened with whitener.

Going back further, I can remember when the Relay radio man first started to hire out his radios. A lot of the neighbours were suspicious and annoyed with him for getting people into debt. My mother said to me, "It's a shame Mrs Patch and the other neighbours don't like the Relay man much." And I replied, "I wonder why they don't like him? They're good radios. We'll keep ours anyway, eh Mum?" The radios were shaped like a square box. They had two dials, one to switch on and one for the two different stations. I think my mother used to pay something like five shillings a week, and the Relay man was responsible for all repairs. She used to keep a card to tick off each week's payment, and if in arrears, she was allowed to pay two or three weeks' money at a time.

In those days, we would get a lot of pleasure from these Relay radios in my mother's little kitchen. We used to listen to series such as *Dick Barton Special Agent, Just William, Mrs Dale's Diary* and *Family Favourites*.

The first school Ron and I went to was Wood Close in Brick Lane. There was a public house on the corner called the Carpenter's Arms. Little did we know at the time that when we got older, we would buy it. We got on well with all the other kids and teachers at Wood Close School, and at our next one, Daniel Street School, which we moved to at the age of twelve.

My favourite subject was English, and Ron's was general knowledge. We used to play football and we did boxing for the school. But our early schooldays were disrupted by the war. We were evacuated to the country for a time.

Both Ron and I have loved the countryside ever since, especially Suffolk. In the war years, we stayed at a place called Hadleigh, near Tring, where there were big fields of red poppies and a mansion owned by the Rothschilds. We used to play in the grounds there with the frogs from the ponds and wish that one day we could own a place like that. Twenty-five years later, we did. We bought a mansion and a cottage with eight and a half acres of land in the village of Bildeston, Suffolk. Our mother had to sell it when we got arrested.

When the war began in 1939, my dad went on the run from the army. He was eventually discharged twelve years later when he and thousands of others received their amnesty from the Queen. Ironically, Ron and I were on the run from the army when Dad received his amnesty.

He deserted the army because he had decided it was more important to feed his children, Ron, our elder brother Charlie and me, than it was to serve in the Royal Artillery. Also, he had never worked for a guvnor in his life.

I can remember the local police who would call regularly at Vallance Road to try to arrest him for desertion, particularly a sergeant by the name of Malcolm. We called him "Humpty-Back" because he had a slight hump. In the early hours of one morning, the police, led by "Humpty-Back", got Ron and me out of bed in our pyjamas. They took us downstairs, proceeded to look in the coal cupboard for Dad, and then asked us questions. Ron and I answered, "We have not seen him, our mother is getting a divorce from him." She had rehearsed this dialogue with us earlier. We were only about six or seven at the time. Ron and I used to hate the police for waking us up in the early hours of the morning.

Another time, they looked in the back yard for Dad. He was hidden in the little toilet and one of the coppers went to see if he was there. The copper had his hand on the door when he suddenly changed his mind and said: "I doubt if he would hide in there."

Dad used to climb over the back wall to get into the yard of the house next door, to freedom. This house was where my Aunt Rose lived. Sometimes he would then clamber into the yard of the next house where my Aunt May lived, and occasionally he would go as far as the Connors' house at the end of the block. Ron and I found this very exciting.

Aunt Rose and Aunt May were my mother's sisters. My mother's brother John Lee lived in the café he owned on the opposite side of the road. His wife, my aunt Maud, used to run the café. She sold delicious meals and the most wonderful fairy cakes, which she made herself. Transport workers would fill the café every day of the week. John also drove a huge coach as part of his occupation.

On one occasion, the police called and Dad was unfortunately trapped in the house because they had covered the entrance to my Aunt Rose's. John Lee spotted the situation from across the road and drove his car to the kerb at number 178. Dad leapt into the car and John sped away.

Another time when the law came, Dad just managed to crawl

beneath the sink which was hidden by a curtain trailing to the floor.

Once, they caught him and he was sentenced to nine months in a detention guardhouse somewhere in the West Country. I remember my mother would send money to him, concealed at the bottom of a Shredded Wheat box which was used to wrap food parcels in. This money Dad would use to buy cigarettes and things. It was, of course, illegal dealing. Another time he was caught and placed in the guardhouse at Woolwich. He escaped to rejoin my mother.

At times, the old man would stay at the house of his friend Bob Rolfe, a South London pickpocket and racing man, just past Camberwell Green. My mother would take us to see Dad there and, on these secret trips, we would carry his clean and dirty washing to and fro.

It was deep-rooted in Ron and me at a very early age to be rebellious, because of the police hounding and searching for my father. But although I have always been anti-authority, through my dad's teachings I have also been a royalist and have never had anything against the upper class. This is because my old man always spoke well of them. He would always say that "royalty can't help being born into their way of life no more than we could", and he would go on to say that we were a lot happier than they were.

He used to teach us that there's good and bad in everyone, in all walks of life and different nationalities. He was a good man. He was always kind to the old people. He used to come in the pubs and buy all the old people drinks and give them money. We had our differences with him, but we loved him also.

When Ron and I would go with the old man on the knocker in the suburbs, buying old clothes door to door, he would always tell us to do two things if the lady of the house answered. First, stand well back from the door so that she would feel comfortable and not afraid and, secondly, always call the lady "madam" in a quiet voice.

The old man was considered by most in the old clothes game to be the best in this particular line of work, and the same could be said when he used to go buying gold and silver. He taught Ron and me these trades, too, and I used to revel in the learning.

During these times, the war was never far away from our daily lives. One morning, Ron and I were asleep at about 8 am in the little upstairs room overlooking the back yard where we slept together in a double bed, when there was a loud bang. We were both slung out of bed on to the bedroom mat. The whole house shook and little things were blown out of place all over the rooms. Black soot blew down from the chimney, and my mother came running into the bedroom and took us both downstairs. My Aunt Rose came from her house at number 176 to see if we were safe, and my Aunt May, from number 174, ran in, too.

There was a lot of excitement. Everyone was telling each other that a rocket had dropped just underneath the railway arch, half-way down Vallance Road, and demolished a complete block of flats with one strike. Many people had been killed instantly while asleep in their beds. I can remember one was a little dwarf who everyone used to like. There were many injured, some trapped beneath the rubble. Rescuers were working with their bare hands in an attempt to free them.

Some days later, the Queen, who is now the Queen Mother, visited the scene of the disaster and Ron and I stood just a few yards from her. She was wearing a pale blue dress, and looked really lovely.

Another time, I saw a doodlebug in the air over Vallance Road. I watched as its engine cut out and it toppled out of the sky and exploded. It made a lot of noise before the engine cut out, and the following silence of this black object in the air was quite sinister and frightening. The wailing of the air-raid sirens always had a sense of emergency and danger, but with the doodlebugs and rockets, there was little warning. They just appeared in the skies.

I also saw dog-fights between Spitfires and Messerschmidts, and a common sight was the air-raid balloons which looked like silver monsters. They reminded me of elephants with their big ears.

I saw London burning by night, a spectacular sight. St Paul's Cathedral was lit up in the distance, and the city looked quite

...us to me in the face of its biggest adversity. There were ...s of smoke coming from the burning buildings, and fire ...gade ladders were zooming up the buildings to rescue people. ...could see firemen at the top of the ladders directing the huge hoses on to the fires. Fire-engine bells were clanging all over London, and searchlights were scanning the skies for the planes. It seemed London was fighting to stay alive. Though I was just a young kid, I could still see the full drama being played out as though London was a huge stage.

The air-raid shelter was all very intimate and cosy to me. When the sirens went off, my mother would grab one of my hands and one of Ron's and race us out of the house, followed by Charlie. We would be caught up in the glare of the huge arc lights roaming and searching round the skies. Sometimes the shrapnel would fall down and splatter into the building walls, leaving craters and indentations. We would hunt and find these different shaped pieces of metal the day after the raid, and also the tin foil which lay around in streamers and was used for some sort of radar for the planes.

On the corner of Vallance Road there used to be a huge lamp-post which seemed to me to be a safety point to reach because it was close to the shelter, a railway arch beneath Bethnal Green Junction railway lines. Amidst the air-raids, we would also be able to hear the clatter of wheels in motion and trains being shunted into position. To me, all these different noises were like music—the music of London; the sounds of a nation at war.

These were days of camaraderie, of closely knit groups of people who were truly at war with the dictator Hitler. In later years, when I had this same type of feeling, I guess we were at war in a way with the establishment. I always considered that drinking and gambling clubs should be legal for the poorer classes as well as for the rich. And it would really needle me that exclusive clubs were run in the West End of London for the rich, while in the poorer areas, these same type of clubs were closed down and said to be illegal. That's another of the reasons why Ron and I were so anti-authority.

Anyway, back at the shelter, inside the huge railway arch were other little arches, each one housing a family. My grandfather Jimmy Lee would build a large stage and put on shows for all of us to watch. On one occasion, Ron got on stage and sang to the music of *Chocolate Soldier from the USA* to loud applause. Another time my grandfather fell off the stage during a singing and dancing act and nearly broke his neck. As is well known, he used to perform his famous white hot poker trick, his walking on bottle-tops, and his tap-dancing, singing and playing of many instruments in these arches. Each time a train ran on the tracks above us, the shelter would shudder, and I would look up from my little bunk and see the whitewashed ceiling shaking.

These stage shows were my first introduction to the theatre, which I grew to love. Years later I went to all the best theatres in London and watched all the great shows. I even went to La Scala in Milan in 1963 to see *Madame Butterfly*.

By day, as kids, we would play games in all the buildings which had been left derelict by the bombs. We also used to play in the cobblestone road of the old London Street.

My nan's house was right on the corner of this street, and in between playing about, we would pop into her house for a cup of tea and a slice of bread or cake. The door of the terraced house was always open, and the main room had an armchair full of cushions. Heavy velvet curtains hung from the window.

There was always a loaf of bread lying on the breadboard with a knife stuck in it, and the teapot would be covered by a woollen tea cosy in pretty colours. Hanging from the ceiling was a long flypaper with flies stuck to the glue, their spindly legs kicking away in their death throes.

Ron and I would finish our cup of tea and continue playing in the roadway, pushing a box-cart about. One of us would be sitting in it, steering with a rope tied to the front wheels, while the other would run pushing it from behind. The front of the box-cart would be shaped into a spike so as to damage any other cart that might smash into it. Most of the kids had spikes on their carts. We had an older cousin, Billy Wiltshire, my Aunt

Rose's son, who would sometimes give our cart a push with both of us inside it, but if one of the large Trumans' brewery carts came along full of heavy beer barrels, pulled along by two or more large shire horses, our elder cousin would think nothing of pushing us beneath the horse and cart.

He was always up to mischief, and when one day I popped my head round the doorway of a bombed building, he slung half a house brick at me, which caught me on the left eyebrow. I had to go to the London Hospital at the top of Vallance Road in Whitechapel Road to get six stitches put in.

This cousin Billy would also get me and Ron to take turns at getting into an empty beer barrel while he gleefully pushed us up and down the cobblestone road, which used to give us a good shaking up. But, in a strange way, Ron and I always felt this would make us more hardy, so we would never complain, though he did upset us another time when we went to Chingford by train.

We were going camping for the weekend with cousin Billy and a friend of ours by the name of Ronnie Gill, who in later years would become a professional fighter. After going to all the trouble of pitching the tent, Billy, for reasons of his own, pulled out the centre pole and the tent collapsed in a pile. He said, "Fuck the camping, let's get back to Vallance Road." He wasn't even content with this. On the way back on the train to Bethnal Green Junction, he took turns with each of the three of us, pushing us beneath the train seats till we were gulping for fresh air. He thought all of this was terribly funny. As I said, he was a lot older and bigger than us, so we had to take it all in our stride.

He used to like a lay-in, as he didn't believe much in going to work, and whenever we would wake him up too early, he would get his own back on us. He would wait for us to use the public baths opposite Vallance Road, in Cheshire Street, and once we were locked in a cubicle, sitting in a hot bath, Billy would climb over the top, grab us by the hair and force us beneath the water until we were coughing and spluttering. As a postscript to this story, I would like to add that he has never been in touch with us in all the time we have been away.

We always used to be up early in the mornings as kids, and especially early when we went to Billingsgate fish market with our uncle Joe Lee, my mother's brother. We were about ten years of age at the time. He would pull up outside 178 Vallance Road at about four in the morning with his huge cart, which had the name "Reece" drawn on the side and was pulled by two big shire horses. The cart would be filled with fish boxes, mostly containing mackerel.

Ron and I would climb aboard the back of the open cart amongst the boxes. My uncle Joe would use his large whip occasionally, and shout the horses on to greater speed. I guess Ron and I thought we were a couple of cowboys. The smell of the fish boxes would be ever present on the back of the cart, and we would wear old clothes so that the fish stains would not matter too much. Fish scales would be strewn all over the bottom of the cart and round the sides, and they would shine in the semi-darkness of the early morning, while bluebottle flies buzzed about the boxes.

Each of these trips was a great adventure for us, riding through the streets of the East End until we reached Upper Thames Street where Billingsgate lay, close to the edge of the river. And there would be the bustle of the market porters with their barrows, wearing white coats and carrying fish boxes balanced on their heads on top of massive leather hats.

I can remember the white seagulls swooping down to the edge of the Thames to get their morsels of fish, and once we were unloaded, we would go with my Uncle Joe into a café in Upper Thames Street where we would enjoy a large cup of hot tea and a cheese roll, among all the other workmen, to take the bite out of the coldness of the early morning. We would look forward to the journey back to Reece's stables in Bethnal Green. My uncle Joe would unhitch the horses, pull them into their different cubicles in the stables, brush them down and feed them oats. Then Ron and I would proudly walk home to Vallance Road, having had a great day.

Around the same time, we used to go out regularly on a pony and cart with a feller by the name of Harry Hopwood. In later years, he was one of the chief prosecution witnesses against us at our murder trials.

Harry and his brother George used to take Ron and me out buying old rags through the streets of London. They would pick us up at Vallance Road with their pony and cart. The cart had a canvas-like shelter, which used to be very cosy on winter days. The Hopwood brothers were like uncles to us, both being in their thirties and close friends of my old man.

Ron and I would sit or stand in the back of the cart with Harry Hopwood, while George would drive the pony with the long leather reins and occasionally give the pony a smack with the whip. As the pony would gallop, the steam from its back would rise, and one could see the sweat on its body and the steam from its hot breath billowing from its nostrils. It would give the occasional snort. I used to love the smell of the leather of the reins and saddle, and the smell of the nosebag in the back of the cart.

We would get to our destination where the four of us would call out, "Old rags", and the kids would come rushing out of the houses with bundles of rags and woollens. From the back of the cart, we would give the kids goldfish, balloons and toys in return for them. We used to keep the goldfish in an old bath.

Very soon the little cart would be full of rags and woollens. Then we would drive away to one of the cafés we used regularly, park outside and have a smashing hot breakfast of bacon, eggs and chips, and plenty of bread and cups of tea.

After that, we would start the journey back to the stables in a little back street of Dalston. It was really comical because the horse would gallop faster on the way back. He seemed to know he was on his way home. George Hopwood would unsaddle the pony and guide it into its cubicle, wipe it down with bundles of hay and give it plenty of oats. The Hopwoods would give Ron and me a couple of shillings each for the day's work.

It seems sad, on reflection, that Harry Hopwood would eventually give evidence against us, but that's human nature.

While I was in Parkhurst Prison, I heard the news that he had died through excess drinking.

Another way Ron and I would earn a few shillings when we were about ten years of age was by hiring out a pony and cart from a stable just off Old Bethnal Green Road. We dressed in our old clothes and cloth caps and would drive the cart to a site where they were digging up the old tar blocks that were part of the road. We would buy sackfuls off the workmen for a few shillings, load them on to the open cart and drive the pony and cart away at full gallop to different streets in the East End where we would sell the tar blocks to the old people for their fuel.

We used to earn good money for this as kids, and the smell of the tar always seemed beautiful to me. We would feel proud pulling up outside Vallance Road with the horse and cart we hired, and we would pop into my mother's house for a cup of tea and a sandwich.

Contrary to general belief, Ron and I never did mind a hard day's work. In fact, we used to enjoy hard physical work of any kind. Later, when we first came out of the army, we both had a job breaking up rock with sledgehammers in the big yard just off the canal in Bow Road.

I will admit that most jobs we had as teenagers, after we left school, did not appeal to us. After about ten minutes of looking around a place of work, like a factory, we would pick up our coats and wander off back to the Red Café, Mile End, which was run by a Jewish feller named Jack Levy. We would sit there drinking tea all day and smoking.

The longest normal job we had, and Ron's favourite, was when we worked six months full-time at Billingsgate at the age of fifteen. Ron was an empty boy, which meant he would gather up empty boxes for his firm in the market. He liked carrying the boxes on his head—it gives you a strong neck, and it's good for boxing. I was training to be a junior salesman.

But we left this job to go with our mother and father to Wisbech, a town in the Fens. There, we went fruit-picking for the summer. The gangmaster in charge was Mr Bill Shippey.

He and his wife Mary are two of the nicest people I have met in my life. They send Ron and me Christmas cards each year.

One evening while we were there, Ron and I pitched a canvas tent by the riverside. Foolishly, we had lit candles in the tent and the next thing we knew, it had caught alight and gone up in flames. We forced ourselves out of the tent and as we fell outside, I got caught up in some tangled barbed wire. It ripped my back open, hence the scar I still have.

I'm reminded of when I was sixteen years of age and on remand at Wormwood Scrubs on a charge of grievous bodily harm on a policeman. On arrival at the Scrubs, I was interviewed by the prison doctor. As I stood naked in front of him, he pointed to the scar on my back and asked if I had ever been flogged. I answered, "No." And the doctor said, "A pity!"

Both before and after the fruit-picking, we had all sorts of odd jobs here and there. Ron was in a tie shop for a couple of weeks; he felt really sorry for the Jewish feller there who had tattoo marks on his arms from Auschwitz.

None of these jobs could ever offer us the excitement we had felt as ten-year-old kids earning a few bob, or the fascinating experiences of our daily lives in Bethnal Green.

I remember when Ron and I used to go to Sigourney's Funeral Parlour in Bethnal Green Road to see our schoolmate Rod Sigourney. His mother, a very attractive divorced woman, used to run the parlour, and whenever she was out shopping, her son would show us the dead bodies in the coffins. It was a gruesome experience, but, being kids, we looked upon it as an adventure. Ron Sigourney had ginger hair, a mischievous face and bright green eyes. He was like the character Just William, very cheeky. Later, he went into the army and I never saw him again.

Funerals are one thing that sets the East End of London apart from the rest of England. When one of a family or a friend passes away, the mourners spend small fortunes on lavish send-offs. They will buy a mixture of the most beautiful wreaths and flowers possible. They will come in all shapes and sizes, and often depict different stages of the dead person's past.

One example was the scene at the funeral of our friend, Tommy Smithson. There was a wreath in the shape of a boxing ring because he had been a fighter, there was one of a ship because he had been in the merchant navy, and there were two huge dice in coloured flowers depicting snakes' eyes because his luck had finally thrown out.

No expense was spared at these lavish occasions. The best cars were used, and I can remember seeing hearses drawn along by proud black horses in my childhood days at Vallance Road.

By the time we were twelve, Ron and I were helping our grandfather Jimmy Kray at his stall in Brick Lane. He lived in a little terraced house off Hackney Road, and he used the stall each Sunday to sell old clothes which he had collected all week on his rounds of the suburbs.

I would collect a barrow for him each week from Great Eastern Street, and run with it to his house at about 8.30 am. My grandfather would welcome me with a cup of tea, and give me three or four digestive biscuits. Then I would climb the rickety old staircase in the house and go into the empty back room where he kept the piles of old clothes on the floor in big black cloth bags. There were old shoes, too, and it was my job to cart them downstairs and load them on to the waiting barrow. Then I would race off along Hackney Road, cutting through all the back streets till I reached Brick Lane. I would park the barrow, unload it and wait for my grandfather to come strolling casually along. He was a well-built man with iron-grey hair.

It was amazing how much money my grandfather collected each Sunday from the sales of his stuff on the stall. I used to stand by it while he sold to those who gathered round. I would keep my eyes open for the many thieves who would steal from us given the opportunity.

I would go for a tea break to one of the many cafés nearby, and I used to love to sit at my table watching all the different people around me eating, drinking and smoking while they talked. My eyes and ears would take in everything. I was already boxing amateur fights at that age, and I remember thinking to myself that one day all these people in the café will read about me. I didn't know then that the pattern of my life would change so drastically, or that I would become notorious, but I did know that I wanted to be known somehow.

After my cup of tea, I would return to the stall and let my grandfather take his turn in the café. We would eventually close the stall down at 2 pm, and I would race the barrow all the way back to his house to unload the clothes that were left and take them back upstairs. Then my grandfather would pay me seven shillings and sixpence wages, which was a lot of money for a boy in those days.

After I'd taken the barrow back and given my grandfather back his deposit money, I'd go back to Vallance Road and share the seven and six with Ron.

Sometimes Ron would do the stall job instead of me. We were very fit in those days. We'd been boxing since the age of ten, and we used to spend our evenings just going walking over at the park. We used to do a lot of walking. I used to lie in bed at nights imagining the great Jack Dempsey, the former world heavyweight champion, travelling from town to town, city to city, throughout the United States in his quest for the title. I used to picture him jumping from the freight trains in his days as a hobo, on the way to the next fight. And I hoped that I, too, would be a champ as I drifted off to sleep.

Our brother Charlie was the first to teach Ron and me how to box. He taught us practically all we knew, with the exception of a few moves that we learned from Charlie Simms and "Kid" Berry. The first time we ever watched any boxing was the day the boxing booth came to Bethnal Green. We were about ten years of age at the time, and the booth was just part of a large fairground on a site where a rocket bomb had dropped at Turin Street. There were roller coasters, dodgem cars and even a giant by the name of Evans. While the loud fairground music played, Ron and I walked over towards a marquee with a stage just beside it. The stage had a large placard with the words "Alf Stewart Boxing Booth" emblazoned on it in large coloured letters. Four or five fighters were standing on a stage, gloved up, with their dressing gowns and boxing boots on. Alf Stewart was also on stage with a mike in his hands, issuing a challenge to the crowd: he would give a pound note to any member of the audience who could last three rounds with one of the fighters. He named the fighters as Buster Osbourne from Bethnal Green, his brother Stevie Osbourne, Les Haycox, and a character by the name of Slasher Warner. Buster Osbourne had a broken nose, as did Warner, and Haycox had a broken nose and cauliflower ears. All looked as though they could take care of themselves.

With the rest of the crowd, Ron and I were finally admitted into the marquee where the fights were to take place. The most exciting fighter of them all was Slasher Warner. He wore black tights and had a magnificent physique. Alf Stewart introduced him into the ring as a bookmaker's bodyguard, and said, "Excuse him if he doesn't fight by the rules!" He won his fight by a knockout in three rounds, and the fighting of the night made Ron and me really excited. We were both red in the face.

During a break between the contests, Alf Stewart asked over the mike if any of the audience would like to get up into the ring and fight for a few shillings. Ron and I jumped at this offer, climbed into the white square ring with the arc light blazing on it, and said we would fight each other.

The crowd were in good humour and clapped and cheered us on. We stripped to the waist and pairs of battered, torn gloves were laced on to our hands. We fought three furious rounds. Ron had a busted nose which was bleeding, and I had a bruised cheekbone. We were sweating with excitement, and Alf gave us seven and six between us. Ron and I ran all the way home to Vallance Road to tell my mother and my Aunt Rose about our introduction into the ring. We felt really proud, and imagined ourselves as paid fighters.

In later years, we got to know and to become friends of all those older fighters we saw on the stage of Alf Stewart's booth on that night, with the exception of Slasher Warner who we did not get to meet. I'm sad to say that, many years later, I was walking down the Roman Road when I saw a grey-haired man with a sprightly walk, a broken nose, but with a bowed head, walk into the kip-house. It was the same Slasher Warner. I felt sad at his plight, and seeing him evoked memories of yesteryear. I could still see him on the stage with his magnificent physique, when his fighting had stimulated Ron and me so much, but, alas, youth is not eternal. I really wanted to follow him into the kip-house to give him some money, but though I looked into the passageway, I could not see him and I missed the opportunity, which I regret to this day.

From the day of the boxing booth onwards, Ron and I worked hard at our training. At the Robert Browning boxing club, our main trainer was Charlie Simms. He would spar with anyone, professional or amateur. Even though he had cauliflower ears, a broken nose and scar tissue across the eyebrows, he was a really good defensive fighter. He only weighed about ten stone seven pounds, yet he would spar with any fighters, even heavyweights. He taught Ron and me, who were lightweights, all he knew.

Tommy McGovern, who became a lightweight professional, used to train at the club regularly. Joe Louis, the heavyweight champion of the world, said that McGovern was the best amateur fighter he had ever seen.

Ron and I also had the pleasure of sparring at the club with Dickie O'Sullivan from Finsbury Park, who was a flyweight champion of Great Britain as an amateur and professional. He told us that he would swear and curse his opponent all the way from the dressing room to the ringside to psych himself up into an aggressive mood.

Once, Ron and I were chosen, with some other kids from the club, to go and box on a Saturday morning on the stage of the Trocadero Cinema in Bermondsey. A large audience of screaming kids watched Ron and me put on a boxing exhibition in a makeshift ring. This was during the time of Saturday morning cinema for the under-fifteens.

As time went on, we joined other clubs—the Webb Boys Club, the Oxford House Club and the Repton Club in Bethnal Green. John H. Strachey, the former welterweight champion of the world, was at one time a member of the Repton, as were other world champions.

During our boxing days, Ron and I were privileged to spar with various champions. One day at Bill Kline's gym in Great Portland Street, Ron had the gloves on with Rolly Blyce who was featherweight champion of Trinidad. Ron's trainer, Harry "Kid" Berry, had to physically pull Ron and Rolly apart after three rounds because they were so ferocious, even though they wore 16 oz gloves and headgear.

Also at Bill Kline's gym, at the age of about sixteen, I had the gloves on with Ron Barton who was light heavyweight champion of Great Britain. I was sorry to read recently that he had an operation for a brain haemorrhage.

We sparred a couple of rounds each with Terry Allen, the flyweight champion of the world, at a gym in Islington when we were about fifteen. He was a chain-smoker, who, after his training, would lie on his dressing table sweating, and smoke one cigarette after another.

Ron and I also boxed a few rounds in Kline's gym with Ben Valentine who was middleweight champion of the Fiji Islands. He was a good man, and I recently wrote to him at an old people's home.

I once had the gloves on for three rounds with Freddy Mack, the coloured heavyweight, at the Clark Brothers' gymnasium in Tottenham Court Road. He used to have a bald shiny head and was a southpaw, which meant he was left-handed and so very awkward.

We turned an upstairs room at our house in Vallance Road into a gymnasium, and used to spar about. Many of our friends would come round, all the boxing kids from the neighbourhood, and we used to knock the life out of one another. We would get up at six in the morning to go running or walking, keeping fit.

The first famous people we ever met were boxers. There was one feller by the name of Ted Covenie. He came from Australia, and one day when we were about ten, our Aunt Rose took us to meet him. We shook hands with him.

Then there was Josef Ashal, a Jewish boxer from the East End, who was at one time a British champion. Our father took us to meet him in Petticoat Lane when we were about twelve years old. He was in a wheelchair, paralyzed from the waist downwards.

At the time, there used to be cards in cigarette packets with pictures of all the famous boxers, and we had one with him on it, posing in his tights. We gave it to him and his face lit up. When he smiled at us, we saw that he had all gold teeth in his mouth. We were so proud to meet him.

We also once met, when we were about twelve, the great fighter from Belfast, Rinty Monaghan, and he gave us an Irish shamrock buttonhole which we still have. It was at Solomon's Gym in Windmill Street. He was a great character. He used to sing after fights.

Also in Solomon's Gym we met the great fighter Freddie Mills. He used to give us money to go to the chemist's and get the bandages for his hands when he was training. He used to call everyone "cock". He committed suicide, in the end.

By the time Ron and I were fifteen, the local newspapers were starting to write about us. In the winter of 1948, I won the London Schoolboy Boxing Championships, after having been schoolboy champion of Hackney. I was a Great Britain School-boys finalist. In 1949, I became the South Eastern Divisional Youth Club Champion and the London ATC Champion. Ron also won Hackney schoolboy and London junior champion-ships, and a London ATC title.

I remember one night in 1948 when we were members of the Repton club. Ron was inside the club, and a film director came round and said he needed extras for a film called *The Magic Box*. Ron and another boy called Shaun Venables put their names down, and the following week went to Ealing to do the job. Ron spotted another extra named Jack "Kid" Berg, a fighter who we really admired and who also came from the East End. Ron didn't get to meet him on that occasion, but many years later when we had two drinking clubs in the East End, the Double R Club and the Kentucky, we met "Kid" Berg and became great friends of his.

At sixteen, Ron and I were becoming notorious in the East

End of London, mostly because we had our own gang, and we had been barred from most of the cinemas and dance halls in the areas round East London as a result.

We used to keep choppers, machetes, knives, swords and all kinds of weapons beneath the bed that Ron and I slept in at Vallance Road. It was a very rough area, Bethnal Green. There were a lot of gang fights, and we had to have weapons of some kind. Ron and I usually always had a knife on us.

We got our first gun off some criminal at this age. Ron always guessed that he would shoot somebody some day. He guessed he would have to. Before long, we had an arsenal of guns, but these were sometimes a nuisance. If the law raided the house, we would be in trouble for the guns, whereas they couldn't do anything about the knives and swords.

We would periodically have to get one of our kindly neighbours to shift the guns to a different house, if we thought we were going to get a turn-over by the law. We would place them in a shopping bag covered up with tins of food or whatever. It was like one big conspiracy, as though our neighbours saw the police as the enemy, just as people would in an occupied country. Though, years later, many people turned Judas on Ron and me, there were many good people who would not think of uttering a word to the police against us.

One day Ron had a brainwave, to stop the constant nuisance of moving the guns. He took a loaf of bread out of the wooden safe where it was kept, and with a knife, he dug a hole through the middle. He then placed a little silver revolver, which was one of our arsenal, into the loaf of bread and pressed the bread he had taken out of the middle over the gun. He then placed the loaf back into the wooden safe.

As Ron said, it was an ideal place to always keep a shooter handy in case we ever needed one. What one must take into account is that in gang warfare in London through the years, gangs had at times attacked their rivals in their own households, sometimes even when they were in bed, and Ron and I were determined this would not happen to us. We had no intention of being caught unawares.

We had been brought up in an area of violence, where one would listen to various tales revolving round it. One story I recall hearing when I was just a boy was that of a paranoid gangster who, when he slept, would always place newspapers all around the floor so that he would hear the rustle of the papers if any intruder entered his bedroom.

It was tales like this that were impressed upon the young minds of the kids in Bethnal Green and the other areas of the East End. And it helped to keep all of us on our toes for the rest of our lives, even if it had the effect of making some a little paranoid and jumpy at any strange noises throughout the night.

One is the product of the environment one is brought up in, and it was not the fault of the parents in these areas either. They had heard the stories, too; they could hardly advise their kids to ignore noises in the night. Ron had listened just as attentively to these tales when he was a boy, hence the silver revolver in the loaf of bread.

We had already been in trouble with the law. At the age of sixteen, we were charged with GBH on three people, Dennis Seigenberg (who was later convicted of killing a fruit-machine operator), Walter Birch and Roy Harvey. This followed a rival teenage gang fight involving bike chains and coshes outside a dance hall in Mare Street, Hackney. Some months later, we were sitting in the Number 1 court in the Old Bailey before Judge McClure. At the closing stages of the trial, our friend Rev. R. N. Hetherington stood as a character witness for Ron and me. We first met him when we were twelve years old. At the time, he lived in Bethnal Green Road. He invited us to his small youth club, and we were all soon running errands for him and listening to his words of advice. At the end of the trial we were acquitted of the charges.

Our second bit of trouble was when we were given probation for assault on a policeman.

When we were seventeen years of age, Ron and I turned professional as lightweights, weighing nine stones and nine pounds. We made headlines in the papers as twin brothers who won their debut fights on the same night at Mile End Arena,

London. I was fighting Bob Manito from Clapton, and Ron's opponent was Bernie Long from Romford.

I had seven professional fights over the next year or so, before we were called up for the army, and won them all. Ron had six. He won four and lost two. Our last fights were in the Royal Albert Hall.

Sometimes today I'm asked how Ron and I can cope with our notoriety. I can only answer that we have grown so used to it over the years that the almost daily occurrence of seeing our name in print does not affect us at all. It's become a gradual process over the years, since Ron and I first had a write-up in the local *Hackney Gazette* for boxing each other when we were twelve.

A few days after that early amateur bout, the *Daily Mirror* newspaper took our first pictures. They came to Daniel Street School, and we wore boxing gear and posed for the photographs. Since those days, not a year has gone by without us being mentioned in the newspapers, local and national, for some reason or other. Of course, a lot of our notoriety came about by word of mouth.

I can remember going to Gray's dance hall in Finsbury Park one night when I was just turned eighteen, only a few months before the army. I got into conversation with someone while we were listening to the records that were playing, and this kid about the same age as me said, "Where do you come from?" When I told him Bethnal Green, he asked, "Have you heard of the Kray twins?" And I said, feeling a little embarrassed and trying to be as modest as possible, "I am Reggie Kray." He looked shocked, and said he expected me to be about six feet tall.

Even by this time, Ron and I had a reputation in London as young villains. We were following in the footsteps of so many others from East and North London who had turned to villainy as a way of making money.

CHAPTER 2

CAREER OPPORTUNITIES

We did everything in our power to get chucked out of the army. Looking back, I feel that National Service could've been a good way of life, though I do not agree that there is any reason for two nations to go to war at the expense of young lives.

Despite all our efforts, however, we remained stationed at the Tower of London when we weren't either absconding or being punished in detention cells for absconding. Early on in our army career, Ron and I were imprisoned in a guardhouse which was situated in one of the towers of the Tower of London. We were quite proud to have joined the likes of Anne Boleyn and others who had been imprisoned there centuries earlier.

One little corporal by the name of Smith, who was guarding us, was really terrified at the thought of ghosts, so I used to play on this and frighten the life out of him in the early hours. I would pretend to be asleep in my cell, and would slip my hand out from beneath the blankets and give three knocks loudly on the wall. I could hear Smith outside, scurrying out of his chair. He would switch on my cell light and say, "Is that you knocking, Kray?" I would remain silent, and then repeat the procedure some time later.

One time, Smith unlocked my cell door and came in. I pretended to wake gradually, and I could see he was worried and nervous. Smith said, "Do you fancy a chat? I don't feel like sleeping myself."

I said "Yes, even more so if you make a nice cup of tea."

He complied with my wish, so we had a cup of tea and a chat about the ghost he was sure was still lurking in the towers. I assured him that I, too, had heard footsteps and knocking in the night, and this made the corporal even more agreeable towards me.

Once, during my time at the Tower, I was in my barrack room when I decided that they might throw me out of the army a bit quicker if I made out to hang myself and got them to think I was some sort of nutcase. So I figured a plan of campaign and sorted out the help of another young recruit. First of all, I wrote out a last note stating that I could not stand army life any longer. Then I got a cord from the kit bags and made a noose. I left the note on my bunk and tied the noose to the ceiling by standing on a table. I told the young recruit to rush off to the NAAFI and to tell the first sergeant or corporal he came across that he had seen me tying a noose. I stood on a table and made myself go white in the face—I'm not a bad actor when I want to be. I positioned myself, holding the rope and noose in readiness for the door to come bursting open, when I would be caught in the act.

The recruit came in with a sergeant, but to my dismay, he only asked me a few questions and gave me a couple of Aspros, saying, "You'll be OK, son," when, at the very least, I had expected a full medical inquiry.

So I hatched another scheme. I was going to become a migraine sufferer, which I hoped would get me chucked out of the kate (kate being an expression used in those days to mean army).

I knew that victims of migraine suffer flashes before the eyes and have blinding headaches followed by bouts of sickness. I thought that before I told the doctors my new tale of woe, I would spend a week with as little sleep as possible, so that apart from acting the part of a patient, I would also look like one. At the time, I was in the guardhouse at the top of the tower, so I would clamber up to the window slats and look out at Tower Bridge until the early hours in my bid to stay awake and cultivate an unhealthy appearance. Cigarettes allowing, I also chain-smoked, thinking that a few coughs would heighten the headaches.

By the time I was taken to see the head specialist at Mill Hill army headquarters for the medically sick in Edgware, I did not look at all well. There were more trips to Edgware but, alas, I was still A1, fit enough for a Royal Fusilier.

Some of my favourite memories are of the days Ron and I spent on the run from the army. One of our favourite haunts was Wally's Café, beside a bus station in Hackney. The café itself was in the front room of an old house. Nearby was a large playing field, which was called London Fields.

Apart from all the villains in the area using the café, the bus drivers and conductors from the depot next door were customers. The owner himself we all knew just by the name of Wally. He was a likeable feller, about five feet eleven, with blue eyes, fair hair and a large nose. Some of those who used to frequent the café were larger-than-life characters, such as the villain Tommy Smithson, whose funeral I mentioned, who would later be shot dead by Maltese gangsters. Then there was Benny Robinson, a thickset blond-haired feller whose brother had been hung for taking part in the robbery and murder of a jeweller in Bethnal Green Road. Another customer was Billy Bellamy, one of a half-caste family, who was brought up in the Hackney area and who was more Cockney than anyone I knew.

We had previously learned a lot from Bob Rolfe and other friends of my father. Now it was really interesting for Ron and me to watch all these villains and thieves chatting at the different tables while we had our regular meal of steak and chips smothered in sauce with slices of bread and butter.

One time, Ron and I had nowhere to sleep, so Wally said, "When I close up later on, you can sleep here. I'll leave the keys with you. You can use the kitchen to make yourselves some tea and sandwiches, but keep the lights out in the front room as the law go by regular." Wally knew we were on the trot from the army, but he did not mind putting us up and looking after us. We never forgot this kindness and repaid him in our own way years later, for instance by installing machines in his café.

The night we stayed there, a copper who was on patrol passed by the café and shone his torch through the window. Ron and I hid in the coal cupboard at the back of the café, and after staying there for a while, suspiciously, the copper moved on. Ron and I then enjoyed a cup of tea.

Billy Bellamy was a kleptomaniac. He would regularly steal a single-decker red bus from the station next door to the café, and take us all for a ride through the streets of the East End, dropping Ron and me off at Vallance Road. There would always be someone to play bus conductor, too.

Billy Bellamy also took Ron and me thieving with him on a few occasions. There was a goods yard over Islington way, and Billy had cased the place. He said we would screw it.

There were cartons of stuff in the yard. The only trouble, he said, was that there was also a large bull terrier in the yard, but he wasn't afraid of that. We went to the yard in the early hours, and whilst we waited outside the fence, Bill climbed over into the yard. He disappeared out of sight, and we heard the dog barking in the distance. He eventually returned and tossed over three or four barrels of cloth which was for making suits with. He then clambered back over to us, and we scurried off into the darkness with our loot. We hailed a taxi which drove us to Queensbridge Road, just off Hackney Road, and we went into Bill's mother's little terraced house.

We often stayed there when we were on the run, and we had some smashing times. They used to have parties. Billy used to sing the song *My Mother's Eyes* while another of his relatives would play the accordion. They were a really loyal family, and Mrs Bellamy, the mother, wrote to Ron and me in Parkhurst right up until her death.

The night we came back with the bags, we had several young Bellamys flying round the house helping us to measure the cloth, which we sold the next day.

This and similar little escapades helped us to get a few quid, and even though it wasn't much, it gave us a meal.

The people I have mentioned so far were at least ten years older than Ron and me, but others in the same age group used the café too. All the notorious Nash family from North London used it. So did their pal Ron Diamond who, in his teens, had a gang called the Diamond gang. There were many others, and they were a rough bunch with convictions between them for robbery and acts of violence. A lot of army deserters went there, too.

The guvnor of the manor then was Tommy Smithson. He could really have a fight. He was about thirty years of age, and was well-known and respected throughout London. He came from Hackney, and was five feet ten with an athletic build. He was good-looking in a rugged way, with a slightly broken nose, high cheekbones, good teeth and brown eyes. He had spent many years in the merchant navy and had fought in the ring as well as on the street. He was a compulsive gambler.

He and another feller, Alf Melvin, once had a fight over at London Fields. Smithson buried a chopper into the skull of Alf Melvin, who was lucky to live. Melvin was about the same age as Smithson. He was an ex-professional heavyweight fighter. He was very broad in the shoulders, had a broken nose and stood six feet tall. Years later, he shot dead his best friend Tony Mulla and then blew his own brains out in a clip joint in Soho, London.

All of these men who lived violently in the fifties and sixties were first and foremost fighting men. They were also men of great pride and none were liberty-takers. They all had their code of honour and had earned any respect due to them by engaging in many brawls, fights and acts of villainy. Nearly all had been to prison, at the very least for short spells.

These men were all part of the world that Ron and I thrived in. They were glamorous days, difficult to describe in that this breed of men seems almost extinct today. But then, I have been in exile for many years, so I am a little out of date. They tell me that Lenny Maclean, who comes from Hoxton, is a throwback to men of that era. Everyone knows that Maclean can have a fight, and he is a regular visitor to Ron.

During my army days, I was court-martialled twice for assault, and Ron and I were also sent to prison for assaulting the copper who tried to arrest us just before Christmas, 1952. We were, at the time, yet again on the trot.

When we finished our month in Wormwood Scrubs, we were taken to a guardhouse at the army barracks in Canterbury to await court martial.

We continued doing all we could to get chucked out of the army while we were at Canterbury. We smashed up the guardhouse, we burnt it out, we wouldn't wear any kind of uniform . . . we were doing all kinds of things.

I managed to steal the NAAFI keys and dispose of them down a drain, and that threw everything into turmoil when they wanted to open up the officers' mess. Another time, I came across the company flag which had also been placed in the guardhouse for safe-keeping. We set to work cutting it into smithereens, and it went down the toilet, so they couldn't hoist the flag on the parade ground. We also managed to sabotage reveille by hiding the bugle.

One of the best laughs we had was when Ron and I, along with our friends Dickie Morgan and Ted Bryant, decided that we would climb on top of the guardhouse and have some fun. I had acquired a mouth organ, and although we couldn't play it, I did roughly learn the tune of *On Top of Old Smokey*. So one day when we were in the small exercise yard walking round, and the guards were looking on from a few feet away in the building, the four of us clambered up a drainpipe till we reached the roof.

We sat amongst the tiles, clinging to the old chimney pot while I played *On Top of Old Smokey* on the mouth organ, and the others sang the words. The sergeant and his crew pleaded with us to come down. We refused, but later on we thought of an idea. We agreed that we would ask those below to fetch Corporal Ted Haines. He was a real good old boy, and had done OK by us when he was on duty in the guardhouse. In fact, it was his son, a naval cadet visiting his dad at the guardhouse, who gave me the mouth organ I was now playing. We decided we would let Ted Haines talk us down from the roof so he would get the credit for it.

We shouted out to those below that we wanted to speak to Ted Haines, and after some time he arrived on the scene. He spoke to us in his usual fatherly manner and we eventually climbed down to surrender ourselves back into the custody of the guardhouse. The leathery-faced, barrel-chested Ted Haines had earned our respect because he was all man. I am glad to say he was made up to a sergeant because of his efforts in dealing with us. He had waited many years for that extra stripe.

We were handcuffed to each other wherever we went in the barracks, whether we were going for a shower or to the stores. At one time, tales started coming back to us that a Scotsman called Stewart, a serving soldier working in the NAAFI, had been saying bad things about us, calling us East End trash.

Ron and I were more touchy and sensitive than we are now, so I made up my mind that Stewart would not get away with it. I said to Ron, Morgan and Bryant, "If I see Stewart, I'm going to do him." I didn't have long to wait. One day soon afterwards, the escort handcuffed me to Dickie Morgan and Ron to Bryant. As we went along to the stores, I saw a lorry parked. Stewart was in the driving seat. We drew close to the lorry and I altered my walking direction. The escort—two corporals—changed direction with me. I called up to Stewart in the driver's cabin, "Can I have a word with you a minute?" He stepped on to the foot-rail, down to the gravel below, and turned towards me. As he did so, I smashed a right-hand punch into the area of his eye, which split on impact. Blood poured from the wound, and he said, "What was all that about?" I said, "Keep your mouth shut about us in future." He said, "No hard feelings," and put out his right hand to shake, but I knew it was a pretence, just an excuse to grab my only free hand. I was right, because as I half gave him my right hand, he tried to pull me towards him to butt me. I reacted quickly and kicked him in the bollocks with my right foot. This all happened quickly, and the escort seemed bewildered and frightened.

It may seem hard to believe, but we used to get the escort to take us for a light ale in one of the nearby inns whenever we left the area of the guardhouse. One time, the escort took the four of us to see the medical officer who was a French captain. As we entered his office, the medical officer carried on perusing some notes he had in front of him, as though he were indifferent to our appearance in his office. There was a cup of coffee standing on his table. Ron spotted this, leaned over, picked up the cup, and, all in one swoop, lifted it to his mouth and guzzled back the coffee. The medical officer looked up in astonishment, went blue in the face, and screamed out, "How dare you! This is outrageous! Get them out of here!"

Ron answered, "You greedy bastard, I only wanted a drink . . ."

The escort couldn't get us back to the guardhouse fast enough.

Another day, one of the guards put one of his hands through the wire into my cell to take something from me. I grabbed his hand and pulled him through and we cuffed him up to the wire. He ended up being cuffed up with his own handcuffs on. We used to get up to all sorts of tricks.

The most dramatic of them all was when we assaulted eleven guards and escaped from Canterbury.

It was an Easter Monday, and a lot of the soldiers were on leave for the holidays, except those in charge of us at the guardhouse. We had planned the escape prior to the holiday, and a van was being brought to meet us near the main gate of the barracks, driven by George Hopwood in the company of his brother Harry and my father.

The four separate cells that we were in were located at the back of a wine compound which had a gate. This gate would be opened each time any of us wanted to go out to the toilet in the nearby yard. Behind the wine-compound gate was another gate that led to the main parade ground. My idea was that Ron and Dickie Morgan would ask to go to the toilet on this Easter night and, as they returned, Ron would grab the guard in a judo lock as he undid the gate. We would grab the keys, open the other gate and make a bolt for our freedom.

As planned, Ron and Morgan returned from the toilet. Ron grabbed the guard in a head lock from behind and put the pressure on while I hit him on the chin. I'm sure he was out cold even before I slung the punch, because I'd seen Ron use this grip on occasions, and he knew what he was doing. Ron would be the first person to tell you he half-choked this guard. Morgan grabbed the keys. There was a guard on the next gate, so we knocked him out. We made a run for it, across the parade ground in the darkness, chased by a posse from the guardhouse. By this time, the alarm had gone up.

We got outside the main gate but could not see the van which was supposed to be waiting for us. We were told later that we had looked in the wrong direction. We ran off down the road chased by the guards. At one stage they caught up with us and we had a running battle with them, but managed to disentangle ourselves from their legs and arms and carry on running.

We came to a low wall in a cul-de-sac and clambered over it. We came to a river and waded across up to waist-level in water. We could hear the shouts of the guards in the distance, and see their silhouettes in the moonlight. We safely reached the other side of the river and after walking about a mile, we came across a coal lorry. Ron told Ted Bryant to get up and start the engine. Ron climbed into the cab beside him while Morgan and I got up on to the back of the lorry. The engine spluttered a few times and then the lorry was in motion. We headed for the main road towards London.

We had journeyed for about ten miles when the lorry seized up and flames and smoke came from under the bonnet of the engine. We descended from the lorry a bit lively and had it away on our toes down the road. We were wearing army trousers, white grandad-type vests and army boots, so we stood out in the headlights from passing traffic, even though we had blackened our faces and the vests with mud. We dived into hedges when we saw any vehicles approaching.

We came to three or four cars parked outside a deserted garage, so we stealthily approached and searched them. Unlike the coal lorry, they were minus the keys, but we did find in one of the glove compartments, all fresh and rosy in a brown paper bag, four apples. It was like fate. We greedily and joyfully ate one juicy apple each and continued our trek towards London with a more eager step.

Morgan, who was a comical character most of the time, was forever complaining about his aching feet, but we urged him on like a real sergeant major would have done with real soldiers. Morgan was the sloppiest recruit you ever did see. Years later, he made a statement to the police against Ron and me.

We finally reached Eltham, and as we entered the built-up area, we stood out in our bedraggled state. Even though we tried to shrink into shop doorways, we were very noticeable. We saw four motorbikes approaching, spread out across the road, driven by uniformed police. As they got closer, they rode up on to the pavement, close to us. We whispered to each other that we would give up without a fight, which we did. The police said to us, "We've been waiting for you for some time."

They escorted us to Eltham police station, a new building, and we were put in cells next door to each other and given tea and sandwiches. They were quite polite, and we enjoyed being the centre of attention. They said an army escort would be picking us up. It did duly arrive, an army truck with a number of guards armed with truncheons. We climbed aboard and headed back towards the guardhouse.

Before the ensuing court martial for assault and desertion, we went before the Summary of Evidence Board. Some of our guards were there, giving evidence against us, and we were told that it was open to us, as defendants, to ask questions of the prosecution witnesses in the box, if we wished. Ron said, "Yes, I would like to ask the feller in the box now a question."

The prosecution said, "Certainly, go ahead."

The person in the box was a good-looking soldier. Ron said to him, "Tell me, what soap do you use? You have got lovely skin."

At this, Morgan, Bryant and I collapsed laughing in the dock, much to the annoyance of those sitting on the board, mainly majors, captains and lieutenants.

Ron was in a humorous mood this day, and when another of the guards said he had been knocked to the floor and had had to pick himself up, Ron interrupted and said, "I would like to ask a question."

The prosecution said, "Granted."

Ron said to the young guard, "Tell me, how did you pick yourself up? Did you get hold of yourself and lift yourself into the air?"

Again, we all laughed in the dock.

At the court martial, in the summer of 1953, we were given nine months each, except for Bryant. He got twelve months because he was a regular soldier and we were National Service. I guess the army authorities took the view that they would give us a light sentence because we were useless and wouldn't make soldiers. We were destined to start our sentence in Shepton Mallet prison, the only army prison in the country, with the highest prison wall. All the other army establishments were detention centres. Years later, they were to film scenes from the film *The Dirty Dozen* at Shepton Mallet.

Firstly, though, we were taken by escort to Canterbury Prison to be detained for fourteen days before our removal to Shepton Mallet. This was the first time I had ever heard of soldiers being placed for custodial purposes in a civvy prison. It was feared that if we were left at the guardhouse before we were moved, we would break out again.

On the day we left Canterbury Prison to go to Shepton Mallet, it was Ted Haines who was in charge of our escort. We were driven in a big open truck, and Ted plied us with cigarettes. For our part, we promised Ted we would not try to escape on the way. I often wonder if his son did continue with a naval career, and if he remembers giving me the mouth organ all these years later.

During our stay at Shepton Mallet, one of the sergeants, a

Grandmother Lee

A street party
after the war

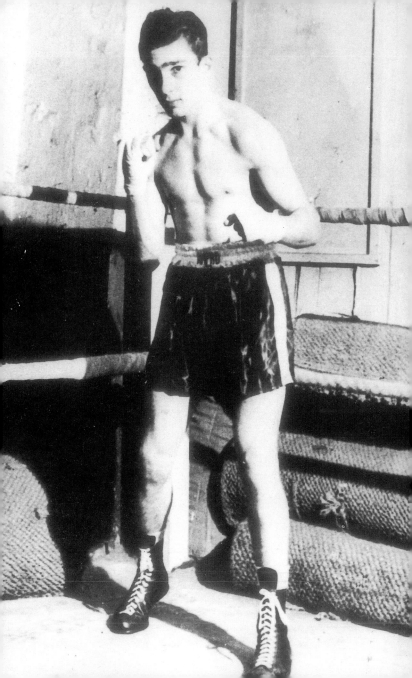

Mum and Dad in the Kentucky Club, 1963

Left: Reg, classic boxing stance, age 16

Reg play-fighting with Grandad, Vallance Road, 1966

Right: Reg and Ron on the run from the army, age 19, 1952

Above: Sulky, Henry Cooper,
Charlie Kray, Reg, and Freddy
Foreman, 1968

Above right: Reg and Billy Hill in
Tangier

Right: Big Pat Connolly, Ron,
Reg, Grandad Lee, acquittal party,
1965

Reg and Frances

screw called Doc Holliday, took us into the "topping shed" where they used to hang people.

He showed us the trap doors and he allowed Ron to stand on the scaffold. There were sandbags on the bottom. It was a bit eerie. Little did Ron know at the time that we would come close to being hanged ourselves years later.

There was another screw there who had a funny eye—he was boss-eyed. He didn't get on well with Ron. One day, Ron was in the boot shop where they had leather knives, and he decided to wind up this screw. He cut his finger a little bit and smeared the knife with blood. He made himself go all white in the face and walked outside with the bloody knife. He yelled, "That's it, that's fucking done it!"

The screw blew his whistle and rushed into the shop where, of course, nothing had happened. He said to Ron, "I thought you'd cut someone."

Ron innocently answered, "I didn't say I'd done anything of the sort . . ."

Johnny Nash and Charlie Richardson, who would in the future head our rival gang from south of the river, were in Shepton Mallet with us. When we'd done our time there, we were discharged from the Royal Fusiliers. So we got kicked out eventually, and we had a result, really. We could have got a lot more than nine months.

We returned to London, and we started to use the Vienna Rooms, just off Edgware Road, as a base. The Vienna Rooms was a second-floor restaurant which catered for businessmen, criminals and prostitutes. Edgware Road police station was directly opposite.

Ron and I were about twenty years of age at the time. Jack Spot, one of the two bosses of the gang which ruled London, and members of his notorious firm, used to frequent the place nearly every evening, as we did, too. Ron and I would sit for hours talking to these characters to learn as much as we could. Many of them became friends of ours.

One was Moisha Blueboy who was close to Spot. He was

Jewish, a villain and a conman. He had done a bit of professional wrestling in his time, and was an exceptionally smart dresser. He was also a brilliant crooked card player.

One night Ron and I were sitting with Jack Spot and Moisha Blueboy when a feller called Jack Pokla came over and said to Blueboy, "I've found a mug from the country who has plenty of money."

Blueboy said, "We'll get him involved in a card game. What's his name?"

Pokla said, "His name is Jeff Allen."

Blueboy told Pokla, "Go and fetch him here for a meal."

Pokla left and came back at about 1 am with a good-looking, well-dressed man in country tweeds, a pleasant sort with twinkling blue eyes. Pokla and Blueboy made arrangements with Allen that a party, which included Ron and me, would go to Jeff Allen's cottage in the country so that Moisha and Allen could have a game of cards. Our group followed Allen's car to a place called Smith's Green, past Southend. We arrived at a pretty cottage in a secluded spot off the main road.

We settled down in well-cushioned chairs while Moisha and Allen played cards. They played for over two hours, by which time Allen had lost a couple of grand—a considerable sum of money in those days. Allen was a good host, and seemed jovial despite losing the card game. He said to Moisha, "If you meet me in the Swan Inn in the village in an hour's time, I will bring you your winnings."

We drove to the inn. Ron and I were waiting eagerly for Allen because Moisha had promised us a few quid of the pickings. But the hour came and went and he had not shown up.

One of the group had had the sense to memorize his telephone number, so Moisha phoned Allen to find out what the delay was. Allen said, "I knew all along I was being conned, and if you come near this cottage, you'll find me waiting with a shotgun." For once, Blueboy seemed lost for words, although Ron and I could see the humorous side of all this. We all drove back to London, weary, but wiser for the experience.

I had remembered the address, and a few days later I told Ron I had decided to go and see Jeff Allen at Smith's Green. I took a train from Liverpool Street and a taxi from the station to the cottage.

Jeff Allen seemed a little surprised to see me. I told him I felt we could do some business together and he invited me in for a coffee. We got on well together, and Jeff went on to become a firm friend of Ron and myself.

Another regular at the Vienna Rooms was Spitzel Goodman, another Jewish feller. He was a dapper little man with thick, black, wavy hair. He had mixed with many of the famous. At one time he was the manager of Primo Carnera, the Italian heavyweight of the world, who was known as the "Ambling Alp" because of his massive size. Spitzel's advice to Ron and me was that if one mixed with class, one would be classy, whereas if one mixed with dirt, one would pick up dirt. Ron and I always tried to remember this sound advice.

Then there was Bar, a coloured feller who had most of one ear missing where someone had bitten him. He had served seven years for shooting and wounding a club owner who had owed him money and not paid it back. He belonged to no gang, but he was very respected and no one troubled him. He owned a famous greyhound called Bar's Choice. It won the Derby one year.

Jack Pokla, who was also of Jewish origin and lived in Paddington, was one character Ron and I were particularly pleased to meet because he was a good money fiddler. He used to buy stolen property, too. We would take in stolen goods and were pleased to participate with him in many crooked deals. A feller by the name of Johnny Stracey, from Manchester, introduced us to Pokla. Stracey used to drive Ron and me about in his Wolseley car. He was small in build, but a very sharp character.

Two other firm friends we made were George and Jimmy Woods. They were both immaculate dressers, and very thickset. George had a scar down the side of his face and a broken nose, which seemed to add character to his profile. They used to wear the most expensive hats and ties. They made front pages when they were sentenced to twelve and ten years for the attempted robbery of a million pounds worth of gold bullion from London Airport. One member of the gang got away. This was Teddy Machant, who also belonged to Jack Spot's gang and frequented the Vienna Rooms.

Ted was born in Upton Park in the East End of London. He could be quite a violent character, which belied his charming manner. He had jet-black hair and the looks of a film star. He also dressed like one. He was tall, with exceptionally long legs, and very agile. At one time, he had an argument with his friend Jacky Reynolds at the Queen's public house in Upton Park. He smashed a broken glass into Reynolds's face, which disfigured him. Reynolds, too, was from Upton Park and a member of Jack Spot's gang. Ron and I became friends with both of them.

Reynolds told me that after the broken glass row, people would phone him to offer assistance against Machant. He refused their help, saying he was still a friend of Teddy's, that it had been just a drunken brawl and that he had no intention of making a comeback against his friend.

Many years later, during my present life sentence, I was sad to read that Teddy Machant was blasted to death at close range by a person with a shotgun. It semed, according to the press report, that he had upset the son of one of his female lovers. Ted died as he had lived: violently. I have many good memories of seeing him placing bets at Epsom Downs on Derby Day, and meeting him on other racetracks. He had been a gambler all his life. It seemed that, in the end, the cards were stacked against him. He was about sixty when he died.

In addition to the Vienna Rooms, Ron and I would regularly frequent Ziggy's Café, just off Petticoat Lane, near Liverpool Street. Ziggy was a smart-looking middle-aged man. He was very stout, and always had a large, fat cigar stuck in his mouth. His wife, who was anaemic-looking, would serve tea and lunches, looking cowed and meek while the gruff Ziggy would oversee the café. He was a well-known character in the East End. A police truncheon would be on show behind the bar. He had grown up in the East End of London along with Jack Spot and his henchmen, so it was only natural that they too would frequent the café. Ron and I found it fascinating to watch them mingling with all the other characters.

Ziggy, like Jack Spot, was Jewish, and both had had many battles with the Fascist element that was rampant in the East End during the thirties. No doubt, the truncheon was available not only for rowdy customers but also for the local Fascists.

The majority of the customers would hang about outside the café each Sunday morning and talk in groups. I particularly remember Sammy Wilde, a coloured feller from the Gold Coast who was a middleweight professional fighter. He was a good-looking man even though he had tribal marks cut down each side of his cheekbones. He used to have a knife in a sheath attached to his waistband, and sometimes would wear a small woollen beret with a coloured tassle on top. He also made appearances on stage as a fire-eater.

But it was Jack Spot and his partner Billy Hill, from Camden Town, who made the most impression on Ron and me in those days. They were the centre of attraction wherever they went. They controlled London as bosses of the underworld.

Spot was a powerfully built man who dressed like a screen gangster. Ron still remembers him as one of the smartest men we ever met, with lovely overcoats, shirts and ties. He was born in Aldgate in the East End and had fought his way up to the top of the ladder. Spot knew that Ron and I were the up-and-coming villains, and he invited us to join in at point-to-point race meetings and at the flat racing at Epsom. He gave us race pitches and introduced us to bookmakers who would work for us along with the clerks we hired. The bookmaker would put up his own money to gamble with and we would keep a dollar in the pound profit, which was five shillings in our currency. We never stood to lose anything. All the underworld characters of the day would preside at these meetings and participate in making a book, alongside their particular bookmakers. Billy Hill had the best stand at these races, which he eventually gave to Ron and me.

We used to park the cars behind the pitches. Ron and I and a friend of ours, Shaun Venables, would have two or three revolvers in a briefcase hidden away in the car, just in case of any gang warfare at the racecourse.

One of the most famous people to be seen at these meetings was a character called Prince Monolulu. He was over six feet four in height, very broad-shouldered, and he wore redskin feathers in his hair. He was one of the world's greatest tipsters. He would sell his tips for a few shillings.

At the races, we would go to the big marquee tents to enjoy cocktails and jellied eels at the buffet. Our friend Bobby Ramsey would drive Ron and me back to London in his maroon Buick.

The Vienna Rooms was always full of new and interesting characters. Jack Spot liked to meet fighters there; he would try to get them to go crooked. I know that he once arranged for Terry Allen, the lightweight champion of the world, to take a dive in the first round of his fight with Dai Dower, when all the money had been placed on Dower. Dower was not part of this deal—he knew nothing of it. Spot also arranged for a fighter to do the same thing in the first round with British heavyweight champion Jack Gardner. Gardner, similarly, knew nothing of the arrangement.

But the man I wanted to emulate most of all was Billy Hill. He was very physical and could be violent if necessary—he wasn't powerfully built, but he could be vicious with a knife. At the same time, he had a good brain, and this appealed to me. I learned a lot by observing the way he put his thoughts into action.

One day, Ron and I, our brother Charlie and our friend Willy Malone were at Vallance Road when the phone rang. Ron picked up the receiver and it was Billy Hill on the line. He said, "Will you come over to my flat as quick as possible."

Ron said, "OK, Billy," and told us, "I think he's got some kind of trouble. Let's get over there."

Ron and I picked up a shooter each and the four of us left, with Charlie driving his car, for Bill's flat in Bayswater. We arrived very quickly. Ron said to Bill, "What's the trouble?

We've brought some shooters." Bill laughed. He left us in the lounge, went into his bedroom, and when he came back, he tossed £500 in brand new notes on to the table. He said, "Take that few quid for your trouble and cut it up between you. I was only testing. I wanted to find out if you would get here fast or if you would blank the emergency."

Another time, two fellers and myself went to the 21 Rooms in the West End. It was one of the most exclusive clubs in London at the time. I believe it was named after its twenty-one bedrooms.

Two doormen in tuxedos refused to let us in. I hit one of them on the chin and he was on the floor. My two mates hit the other doorman and he was on the floor, too. I thought we might get nicked for grievous bodily harm, because I had a feeling one of the doormen recognized me. I also knew that Billy Hill used to get a few quid for looking after the place. So the three of us went to Bill's flat and rang the doorbell in the early hours. I told him the story of the row, and asked if he would check up the likelihood of us getting nicked.

To my surprise, Bill did not seem annoyed that we had hit the doormen, even though he was looking after the 21 Rooms. Instead, he seemed pleased. He phoned Harry Meadows, who owned the club with his brother Bert, and said, "This is Bill. I've just heard that you've had some trouble at the club, and I'm phoning to let you know I've taken care of it. You won't get any more trouble. Just leave it to me. I'll pop in the club to see you tomorrow night.' He replaced the receiver and gave me £300, again in brand new notes. He said, "Take that few quid. It would've cost me more to have hired someone to liven the place up so as to ensure they still need me looking after it." He had a twinkle in his eyes.

The next day, he would go to the club and probably pick up about five grand for preventing further trouble—not that there would be much to take care of in an exclusive place like that. And so us three tough guys from the East End had given Bill just the opportunity he needed to squeeze a few more quid out of the Meadows brothers.

To me, Bill was the ultimate professional criminal. I like to think that in some ways I have come close to emulating him, but in many other ways he stands alone. There will never be another Billy Hill.

The Vienna Rooms was also a haunt for prostitutes who would sometimes mingle with the customers, led by a big blonde called Kate. A Maltese pimp, by the name of Paul, used to use the place. Ron and I robbed his flat once, because we did not like pimps. Tony Mulla, who had pornography shops in Soho, would also pop in for a meal occasionally.

At the age of twenty, we were also using a little drinking club in Paddington called Barry's. It was owned by Dave Barry who had a reputation as a fighter on the cobbles. At one time he hit someone on the chin, and killed him. He was sentenced to eighteen months for manslaughter. He was a very likeable person and a good money-getter. We had been introduced to him by our friend Billy Jones.

Billy, who was about forty, came from Watney Street in the East End and when he worked for a living, which wasn't very often, he was a gangmaster at the docks, deciding which men would work which shifts to load the cargo on to the boats.

Dave, Billy, Ron and I would plot various schemes to obtain money by false pretences. Billy found a sucker down in the dock area of the East End who was a bookmaker. We would place bets with the bookmaker which we would call after time. Either Ron or I would use a phone near the café where the bookmaker took bets. We would get the result of a race just a minute after it finished. We would then saunter to the café where Billy was waiting with a cup of tea, give him a pre-arranged signal to tell him the winner of the race, and he would then place a bet and, a while later, claim his winnings.

We had another racket which we arranged with a crooked doctor. It involved getting people aged eighteen and nineteen exempted from National Service. It was usually their parents who paid us the fee for this service, and we would evaluate the fees according to the wealth of the parents. We split the fee with our doctor and he would pay part of his share to a doctor in charge of the examinations at the medical base in Mill Hill, Edgware. This was quite a lucrative enterprise which lasted until the end of National Service. All parties concerned were happy with the results, especially the young kids who could resume their ambitions without the interference of National Service. Everyone in the East End despised it.

Another racket we had was getting what we called dockers' tickets or books, which we sold for a fee. Again, we would evaluate a client according to his financial position. We would obtain dockers' books, which would then enable the customer to work as a docker at the quayside, loading boats and barges. They were paid high wages, and the actual working hours were very short. Most of the dockers had all day to themselves.

We also used to earn money from watches which were smuggled in from the dock areas without being cleared through customs. These watches were obtained duty-free, leaving leeway for a large profit.

We began stealing lorry-loads at this time, too. We stole loads of furniture, even a lorry-load of sacks, and another time a load of fruit—anything we could get our hands on. We would drive them to a pull-in in the country which was on an old farm. There we would unload and get paid out. Three other people joined Ron and me on these trips: Dickie Morgan, Dickie Mountain and Ron Bennett.

One time we went round a bend on a country lane and half the load of boxes of apples shot off on to the road. We had to stop the lorry to reload. I can remember unloading the lorry-load of sacks, too. It gave us blisters on the fingers.

But I used to like the scene of unloading in the early hours of the morning when the dawn was creeping in and the dew was on the grass. There's nothing like hard work to make you feel good.

The farmer who used to buy our stuff once asked us to take an open lorry to an air base nearby, which was patrolled by American redcaps carrying guns. We were to steal some aeroplane parts made of valuable metal which were lying there. We did manage to do this.

We stole so much that the local newspapers reported that a black-market gang was operating in the East End.

By nights, in these times, we'd go to parties and pubs as well as the clubs I have mentioned. Every so often we'd go to the cinema. Ron particularly liked *Lawrence of Arabia*, and anything about Churchill and Gordon of Khartoum. He thought they were great, brave men. He also used to read about Nelson and Genghis Khan who thousands of years ago had a law among his tribes that if anyone interfered with a woman or child, he'd kill them.

We used to entertain a lot of friends at home in Vallance Road. The police were parked outside the house once, watching it, and Ron took them out a cup of tea. They said, "Thanks, Ron. What have you got in there? A fucking dance hall? There's enough people going in and out."

Over the years, Ron and I were in so many battles together that I've lost count, and forgotten the majority of them, but one fight I will always remember took place at the Coach and Horses public house, in Mile End Road, when we were about twenty.

We went to the Coach and Horses with a feller by the name of Pat Butler who was on the run from a borstal. The three of us were standing close to the bar having a drink of brown ale, and there was a group of dockers standing nearby. We did not know them at the time, but they seemed to know us because they started to make remarks about us, using our names. Ron and I knew that they were deliberately having a go at us. I quietly told Butler to leave the pub and that we would see him the next day. I didn't want to see him get caught by the police when the trouble started. What the five dockers did not take into account was that Ron and I could talk in our own code if we needed to. Within their earshot, I spoke to Ron in code and said we should do the five of them. Ron agreed.

I made up my mind which one I was going to start it with. He was over six feet. Ron was going to start with another of the same size. I walked out of the bar into the street, turned left and entered the private bar which led back into the public bar where the dockers were. I had a glass in my hand. I came up behind the six-footer, and smashed him with a left hook with the glass protruding from my hand. He was out cold on the floor. Ron smashed the other six-footer in the face, and the battle was in full swing.

I grabbed the six-footer who was still standing by the throat, and Ron hit him with a chair repeatedly. This all happened very quickly. Ron and I were also fighting with the other three. In the end, the five of them lay cut and bleeding on the floor, and the bar, which had been packed with people, was almost empty. They had all scattered.

Ron and I left the pub as fast as possible, and hailed a passing taxi to take us to Vallance Road. We told our parents we had been in some trouble, and if the police called, they should say they didn't know where we were. But if any of our friends wanted to see us, we would be staying at Kate Cripps's flat in Myrtle Street, Hoxton. We got back in the waiting taxi and asked to be dropped a street away from Myrtle Street. We did not trust the cab driver—he might've got in touch with the police after seeing our bloodstained clothing, and, as twins, we would be easily recognized.

We were lucky enough to find Kate at home. She was a very good person who would look after anyone in trouble with the police. We told Kate we wished to stay at the flat for a few days. She could see from the bloodstains that we had been in some trouble, but we had grabbed clean clothes at Vallance Road so we could change.

The following day, the story about the terrible fight in the Coach and Horses was all over the East End, and we knew the names of the dockers we had the row with. They were members of two families from the Bow Road area, and all five had been admitted to hospital suffering from cuts. The two six-footers also had concussion.

Ron and I got in touch with Bobby Ramsey, our ex-pro fighter friend, and the three of us drove in his Buick car to a block of flats in Bow Road to speak to a relation of some of the dockers. We told the occupant of the flat we would hold him responsible if any of the five made statements to the police. But we had no need to worry. All five were very sound people. In fact, they all came to drink in the club which I opened about three years later, and I gave one of the six-footers a job on the door. They admitted to Ron and me that they had been drinking too much on the night of the row, and had deliberately provoked the fight.

We were the same age, twenty, when a more serious incident occurred. I referred to this earlier on when I said that Ron and I came very close to being hanged. At the time, capital punishment was still in existence in Britain.

It all began when Ron and I drove to a club in Tottenham Court Road in the West End of London. It was a club for drinking and loud music, and it was packed out with Africans. We were carrying concealed weapons. Ron had a long knife tucked down the waistband of his trousers, and I had a wooden police truncheon hidden on me. There was no particular reason for the weapons except that most people who frequented such clubs in those days carried weapons. Ron and I were always tooled up anyway.

We bought a drink at the bar and were joined by young Harry Abrahams, a seventeen-year-old Jewish kid who was also from the East End. He was a member of our billiard hall in Mile End which we started running after we got chucked out of the army.

I gave young Harry the money to go to the bar for another drink and while he was there, a thickset African feller of about thirty years of age bumped into Harry and called him a right bastard. From a short distance away, Ron and I saw him grab Harry by the collar and tie, and we strode over to the fracas.

I pulled out the truncheon and hit the African as hard as I could on the head. Blood spurted out from a deep gash on his skull, but he was so strong he never even hit the floor. I must have struck him another three blows with the truncheon, and before I knew it, I just had the handle left in my hand. It didn't seem possible that a wooden truncheon would break on a human head, but it did. I found out later that night, by trying it out, that it was more difficult to break the truncheon on paving stones.

By now, blood was pouring from the African's head, and Ron plunged his knife into his side twice. We decided he had had enough, and left the building hurriedly with young Abrahams in tow. This all happened in a matter of minutes, and just as we got to our car outside, three more Africans came chasing after us. One was closing in on me, so I turned round and hit him on the chin and he hit the ground. Then we were in the car and away back to the East End and our house in Vallance Road. Our clothes were covered in blood, and we knew we had been recognized by some of the patrons of the club. Even at that age we were well known in central London.

In the early hours of the next morning, we answered a knock at the door. It was Bobby Ramsey and a good friend of ours, Lorraine. They had been in the West End, and the word was out and spreading that the Kray twins had seriously injured an African in a club. In fact, Bobby Ramsey and Lorraine told us the African was dead.

It was not a nice feeling to think that we had committed murder and that we would probably hang, but we invited Bob and Lorraine into the house for a cup of tea while we decided what to do about our predicament. Our guests mentioned names of witnesses who could identify us, one being the doorman and another a woman who part-owned the club. We decided the best thing to do was leave Vallance Road, get rid of the bloodstained clothes and set about straightening up the witnesses.

We went to a safe address and contacted a friend of ours called Flash Ronnie who knew everyone in the West End and, in particular, Soho. We made a meet with Flash Ronnie who supplied us with a list of names we needed to straighten out the witnesses. In the meantime, we heard the good news that the African was not dead, but had had a bad operation on his body and skull. The knife wounds had just missed his liver.

We found out that the police had left messages at Vallance Road, saying they wanted to see us at Bethnal Green police station. We made sure by threats and the passing of money that no one would pick us out on an identification parade, got hold of a top barrister and then contacted the police station. We were told to contact West End Central station where we were wanted on a charge of attempted murder.

Our barrister accompanied us to West End Central, and we were placed on an identification parade. We had figured out a couple of moves in advance. Two days prior to the ID, Ron and I had haircuts like the police had in those days, short, with the sides greased down. We had bought two outfits, also like police wear. We did this because normally on a police line-up, they had plain-clothes police mingling with the accused, so we wanted to look as much like coppers as possible, thus confusing the African and other witnesses.

When we arrived, our barrister made sure no witnesses were around the entrance, where they could see us coming in. But just in case, we walked in wearing loud overcoats, coloured scarves and caps, and just seconds before we walked on the ID, we stripped them off to reveal our police-like suits and ties. I even had pens stuck in my top pocket, like some office clerk.

We waited, tensely, on the ID parade for the witnesses to appear, and the first couple, the doorman and the female part-owner, did not pick us out. We drew in sighs of relief, but the big one was yet to come.

After a wait of about five minutes, the African who had been injured was brought into the room, his head swathed in bandages. He was wearing pyjamas and slippers as he limped slowly towards us. He walked past me, but pointed a finger at Ron and another feller on the line-up. I could hear the heavy breathing of the African, and I was trying to control mine. But the ordeal was over for me and Ron because the barrister stepped in and said, "That's enough; he failed to pick out both my clients." The police were not happy, but there was little they could do. Ron and I gave the barrister an extra £50 for his good work, and then caught a taxi back to the 99 public house where we joined my father and his friends for a drink.

The old man was well pleased things had gone so fortunately for us. It was he who had arranged our brief. And that was the time that the hangman Albert Pierrepoint was cheated of his prey. Thankfully, we slipped his noose.

CHAPTER 3

GOOD TIMES, BAD TIMES

In 1957 Ron had just been sentenced to three years. He and two others had been found guilty at the Old Bailey of GBH on one Terry Martin outside the Britannia pub in Stepney. Ron also pleaded guilty to possessing a loaded revolver. I had been arrested and taken to court on the same charge with Ron, Bobby Ramsey and Billy Jones, but I was found not guilty.

It all started at a club called Stragglers, near Cambridge Circus in the West End of London. It was being run by Billy Jones and our old friend Bobby Ramsey who called Ron and me in, for a percentage, to sort out a few fellers who were making trouble there.

A couple of them, who were from the Watney Street dockers gang, took exception to being slung out, and there were a couple of fights in the East End. Things got worse when they did Bobby Ramsey and it finished up with Martin, who was one of the dockers' gang, giving names to the police from his hospital bed. He also gave evidence at the Old Bailey.

Grassing is, obviously, one of the cardinal sins in the criminal code. There are no particular rules laying down what you should do, but there are unwritten laws governing unacceptable behaviour. For example, one should never go with another's wife. One should never cross the threshold at a prisoner's wife's home when calling to give her money for the family, out of respect to the man who is away. Ron and I would always send two of the firm to deliver the money, never one alone. This way no one could say that a member of the firm was making a play for the wife of anyone away in prison. It was also part of the code that one should not have anything to do with pimps— "ponces". We did not steal from the poor, or hurt the innocent or women and children.

Today, both Ron and I regret the passing of yesteryear where one would willingly light the fire for an elderly neighbour. There would be more chance nowadays of the elderly being raped or robbed if they asked for assistance of any kind.

Ron has a very kind side to his nature, even though he's a complex character, often contradictory and eccentric. With brothers, especially twins, one is always tagged as the bad one and the other as good. It was Ron's fate to be tagged as the bad. Just like a coin has two sides, so has the dual side of twins. Some of Ron's early actions formed the basis for this two-sided coin, just as mine did, too.

I've known him to be vicious when necessary. He was once upset by a former friend called George Dixon. Ron took a shot at Dixon with an automatic Luger, but the gun jammed and Dixon luckily escaped. Later on, Ron gave Dixon the bullet that had jammed, complete with the indentation mark from the firing pin.

I remember one evening when Ron and I, "Scotch" Ian Barrie, who was one of our right-hand men, and another friend called John Heibner went to the Green Gate public house in Bethnal Green Road. It was owned by the Bird twins who were friends of ours. They used to have a band playing music each night, and the pub would be packed out with people from all over London. Once, we took Winifred Atwell, the great pianist, to play there, and Lenny Peters, the blind singer, used to appear there regularly. On this particular night it was packed, and Ron was sitting on a stool at the bar, drinking his usual gin and tonic. John and Ian and myself were close by, at the bar. Five loud and aggressive young fellers came to the same area of the bar and ordered drinks. Two of them started to make remarks about Ron as he sat at the bar. This went on for a couple of minutes. Then I saw Ron go white in the face with fury. He suddenly stepped down from the bar stool and struck the loudmouth on his left with a right-hand punch, sending him crashing to the floor, out cold. Within seconds, Ron had turned quickly and hit the one on his right with a left hook. He, too, fell to the floor, spark out. It was like a scene from a cowboy film. The band was still playing and I said to the other three hooligans, "Get your mates out of here." They didn't hesitate. Ron just got back on the stool and continued drinking.

Ron, who was nicknamed "The Colonel", was completely fearless. He proved this at our Eric Street billiard hall when four or five Maltese people from Commercial Road pulled up outside in their car. Two of them entered the hall to demand money off Ron. Without hesitation, he picked up a long sword that he kept behind the bar and chased the Maltese out of the billiard hall to their waiting car. He proceeded to hack away at the car with the sword, smashing the windows, too, before they sped off to safety.

I have also seen Ron's acts of kindness. Later in our career, when we were in Tangiers, he unofficially adopted an Arab in the Casbah. This Arab had once been a very intelligent person, but had been tortured as a political prisoner and was now a down-and-out tramp and beggar. Ron gave him suits and other clothing, looked after him and helped him regain his dignity. Ron is the most loyal of friends, even if at times he has been known to be a bad enemy.

In the Terry Martin row, which sent him to Wandsworth, Ron did not use his gun. But he did use it on another occasion, around the same time, when he shot a docker in the leg for taking liberties at a garage we were looking after. He also shot at and missed Billy Falco, a man he now considers to be one of the nicest friends he's ever had. This happened in the Central, an Italian club in Clerkenwell. Ron was with another feller who was having a fight with Falco. At the time, he was friendly with the man he was drinking with, so he took a shot at Falco. He has since told me, "I'm glad I missed him that night. He's a real gentleman, a smashing feller, and he's done me untold favours. I once owed him money and he wouldn't take it back. He gave it to me as a gift."

With Ron away in Wandsworth I was a little lonely, but determined that I would make progress for both of us during the time he was in prison. I did not have long to wait for a new opportunity. One day, I was on my way to our billiard hall in Mile End, a good business with a regular income—it had fourteen full-size tables—when I was approached at a street corner near Mile End tube station by an old tearaway called David Cohen. He told me that there was a large, empty house in Bow Road which he thought would make a good club. *This* was progress.

As a matter of interest, there was a drinking bar near our billiard hall which was run by Joe Abrahams, an ex-featherweight pro fighter. Cohen said, "I'm sure you can run a better club than Abrahams." There had, in the past, been some animosity between the old tearaway Cohen and the club owner Abrahams. I guess Cohen had this in mind when he gave me the address of the house in Bow Road. I thanked him and said I wouldn't forget him for putting me on to the empty premises.

I made enquiries and arranged to see a big property owner in the Park Lane area. He was a smart Jewish man, and he and I took a liking to each other right away. I told him I wished to open the premises as a club and he said he would have no objections. In fact, he said he would come to the first night. I feel he was impressed with me because I was just twenty-three years of age. We agreed to a specific rent and shook on the deal. I then borrowed the first three months' rent from a car dealer I knew called Johnny Hutton.

I had the place decorated. It had a little stage, a very colourful bar and really good flock wallpaper. I bought the furniture, arranged for a jukebox and had everything ready for opening night. There was just one snag. I did not have enough money to stock up with all the drink I needed.

I phoned my brother Charlie and because I considered blood

was thicker than water, I invited him to be my partner if he would put up the money for the drink. He agreed. I had got the licence and all the necessary paperwork, and I knew the club would be packed out on the Wednesday night it opened. I had a good following.

I was right: we had a full house, and the opening night of the Double R Club was a complete success. I sent a telegram to Wandsworth Prison to tell Ron.

A few months after the opening, one of the Martin family, who were responsible for getting Ron his three years, opened a spiel, which was a gambling club, almost opposite the Double R. I thought this was a liberty, but I decided to turn it to my advantage. I arranged for a fire bomb to be hurled into the spiel and at the same time got myself an alibi. When this was done, the Martin family realized they were on my manor and left the premises.

Their co-partner, an Indian by the name of Anwah, was left in the club. I took over as his partner, and arranged for my friends Georgie Woods and Jackie Reynolds to take care of my interests in the gambling. I also cut Charlie in on the takings. Of course, Ron was a part of all this, even though he was away.

Before long, another building was pointed out to me, also just off Bow Road. I set about getting these premises, too, and again put Georgie Woods and Jackie Reynolds in to start another new gambling club. Of course, Ron and Charlie were included.

This, too, was a thriving gambling club, so with the billiard hall, the Double R Club and two spiels I was kept quite busy. The billiard hall and the spiels were open night and day, and I would travel about from one to the other in one of the many cars I had at my disposal, incuding American Fords and Buicks.

Just a mile away from the Double R Club, a drinking club called the Maryland opened. True to its name, it was situated at Maryland Point, Stratford. I considered this was too close, so a fire bomb also went through the window of the Maryland, and the owners soon came to me, rent book in hand. That was another club to add to the string.

I managed to deal with all of my club problems quickly and efficiently, except for one: Dolly Kray, our brother Charlie's wife (now his ex-wife). She used to stand there, all ladylike, telling everyone it was *her* club and I was just the doorman. I'm not knocking Charlie, but the Double R Club was like a home to me; I was kind of married to the place. I loved every moment, whereas Charlie would stand in the corner with his wife. I was the main host, I really worked at it, and I would do most of the door work myself, which I enjoyed. It meant I could take care of any trouble. If anyone had to be thrown out, I would do it myself. Even though I did have a doorman, I preferred the personal touch. A few rowdy customers could testify that my personal touch was enough.

I have met some really terrible people in my time, but the one with the poorest personality, and looks to match, is Dolly Kray. She was the only person, for want of a better word, who never got on well with my mother, and my mother did try, for the sake of Charlie, to make her welcome into the family. My old man never did like her, right from the start. Ron and I detested her.

I remember the first night she knocked at Vallance Road to show herself. She had a scarf wrapped round her head and her large, protruding nose was peering out at me as I answered the door to her. From that day on, we called her "Snotty Nose" or "Skinny".

Charlie and all the world know now that "Skinny" jumped into bed with George Ince when Charlie was inside doing his ten years after our murder trials.

I read Charlie's book recently where he was on about the ten-year sentence he got being a miscarriage of justice. My opinion is that the judge, Melford Stevenson, did him a favour. It got him out of the clutches of "Skinny" for a few years, and he should be jubilant that she married her lover, Ince, and divorced Charlie. George Ince, who was acquitted in what was known as the Barn Murder trial, was always a slag to me, even though he used to frequent our billiard hall in the late fifties. It was I who first tumbled that he was going with Charlie's wife, so I got hold of him outside the Double R Club and butted him in the face. Ron and I then warned him off the manor of the East End, and he made sure he stayed away.

Years later when I was in Parkhurst serving this life sentence, I was with my friend "Hate 'Em All" Harry Johnson who was doing eighteen years. During this time, there were articles in the newspapers about Dolly Kray and George Ince sleeping together. Charlie was in Maidstone Prison at the time. Harry Johnson said, "I hate anybody who sleeps with another guy's wife, so if I come across that George Ince, I will cut him."

I said, "I would rather you leave it out, Harry. The slag is not worth doing bird for."

But Harry had made up his mind to settle the score for the slight on the Kray family. Ince had just been sentenced to fifteen years in Long Lartin prison, Worcestershire, and just a while later Harry was sent there from the special security block in Parkhurst.

Harry kept his word the first day he got there. He spotted Ince watching a football match. This put him into an even worse rage because Harry hated football—he called it "the poor man's sport". So he left the football field and went to pick up a knife in one of the prison wings. He then returned to the pitch where without hesitation he slashed Ince down the right side of his face. He was charged with malicious wounding and received an extra three years in prison.

At the trial, the judge who sentenced Harry said in his summing up that there were serious undertones in this case. He was obviously referring to the influence of Ron and me over Harry Johnson, but we did not influence him. Having said that, though, I am pleased at the thought that each time Ince has a shave in the mirror, he will remember that one should use the brains in one's head rather than doing what he did: he followed the desire of his lesser assets.

Anyway, back to the Double R Club where I was thoroughly enjoying the routine. Each evening, I would make a point of buying everyone who entered the club a drink and would talk to them. They in turn would buy me a gin and tonic. I was such a good drinker in those days that I would always finish the many glasses of G&T that I had set down in different parts of the club room. I can assure you that was some drinking—all my customers were the best of spenders!

I rightfully looked on the Double R Club as mine. It was the first of its type in the East End of London, a place where a man could take his mother, wife or fiancée for a drink in a respectable atmosphere. On my own, and with Ron when he came out, I would stay out each night until the early hours, drinking with all kinds of people, with my eyes on a few quid. It was Ron and I who made connections with people from all walks of life during our nocturnal drinking bouts. Dolly would ruck with Charlie if he stayed out any later than 11 pm.

We would be spending money going out at nights in search of a major deal which would eventually lead us to a better lifestyle. We were professional money-getters from an early age; the others around us were amateurs. We needed no one else physically or mentally. We carried the rest of the firm for years.

While Ron was in Wandsworth, he seemed OK, but things started going wrong when they transferred him to Camp Hill Prison on the Isle of Wight. He had a breakdown, and after being sent to the psychiatric wing of Winchester Prison, he was certified insane in February 1958. During this period, he was put in a straitjacket—which he tells me "feels terrible"—after hitting a screw. Eventually, he was taken to Long Grove Mental Hospital in Epsom, a place where the behaviour of the other patients became impossible to tolerate. I decided to get him out of there, so I thought up a plan which I rehearsed with Ron a week in advance.

On the day itself, I went to visit him with a few other people. I dressed in a blue suit, same as Ron's, and had my hair cut to the same length. I wore an overcoat to hide the suit. When Ron came in, I gave him the overcoat and sat down with my head buried in a photograph album I'd brought with me, pretending to be Ron while he pretended to be me. Normally, I would go to collect the tea and bring it back, but on this day, Ron went for it, still pretending to be me. He'd been gone for some time when the screw in charge of the ward started looking at me. Eventually he said, "You've pulled a flanker."

I said, "What do you mean?"

He said, "You shouldn't have let him go."

I replied, "It's your job to look after him, not mine."

They had to let me go.

In the meantime, Ron had gone off on the long walk to the car. We'd brought two cars down, one outside the main gate and another one up the road, which is the one Ron got into. And he was free. It was quite an exciting day, really.

But, in the end, Ron decided he had to go back to the hospital. He had more treatment, and in a few weeks was well enough to finish his sentence in Wandsworth. By the beginning of 1959, he was back in the East End at the Double R Club and all our other old pub and club haunts.

One pub Ron never did like was the Blind Beggar in Whitechapel Road, Stepney—the pub where he would later shoot dead George Cornell. It's been renovated since then, of course, but in the old days, Ron hated the sight of the Beggars, and called it a dump. He says today that he must have had a premonition about it.

We used to go to various different pubs, like the Crown and Anchor in Cheshire Street and the Grave Maurice in Whitechapel. It had little private cubicles, and they served lovely beef sandwiches. The doctors from the London Hospital used to go in there.

Ron used to like drinking gin and tonic, but if he was drinking beer, it would be brown ale. He claims a record of fifty-three pints of brown ale in one night. He used to pour it down. Ron, Charlie and I could drink all night and never get drunk. Even the hard-drinking American Mafia men who came to see us in later years were amazed at our capacity for putting so much drink away.

I miss those social gatherings. On a typical night, Ron and I would walk into a public house in the early evening, just the two of us, and take out our phone books. We'd phone our friends in different parts of London, and within an hour, they would all start to arrive in cars or taxis to join us in drinks and social and business talks. They were people from all walks of life, some villains, some bookmakers, publicans, professional and ex-professional fighters and their managers, and business-men, intermingled with a few celebrities.

The publicans used to love us, as we would pack the place out with the best spenders. Sometimes we would have a whip-round and each of us would place a pound note or more in a drinking glass set on the bar. The publican would take the money from the glass until it was empty. Then we would replenish it and order more drinks.

The bar would be full of smoke from cigarettes, you could smell the alcohol all round the room, there would be music from either the piano or the jukebox, and there would be an atmosphere of camaraderie. Ron and I would walk around the bar, together or separately, talking to everyone and making sure they were happy. We'd have conversations about earning money and ways to do it, deals and gangland politics. If we wanted to discuss serious business, we would normally be allowed to use a private room in the pub, but if this was not available, we could always use the private bar, which was quieter.

These gatherings would see a group of forty to fifty people each evening. It's amazing, the value of a good phone book. Even today, in my seclusion, I have three full books of names, addresses and numbers.

The publicans would usually lay on sandwiches, pickles, crisps and peanuts, and once a week, on a Monday, we would get up a list for the "aways". Everyone in the pub would donate some money, according to their means, for the wives and families of those in prison. Some of it would go to help the cons themselves.

Most nights we would, with the permission of the publican, stay behind for some after-hours drinking, and sometimes we would have a party upstairs. If we felt like it, we could always go to a club locally or in the West End of London, and we would leave in a cavalcade of cars. Some of the drivers were, of course, over the limit. The pubs we used, and the clubs, too, would be like car parks outside with a galaxy of different cars belonging to our friends. Even the cars added colour to the procession.

These would be really interesting nights, with all the politics of the criminal underworld involved, and the politics of other businesses, too. We all enjoyed the good music and the drink. It would not be an exaggeration to say that they were times of wine, women and song.

Most people present were good dressers, and all had their own special life stories to tell, all being people of varied lifestyles. I can remember one evening in particular when the ballad singer Kevin O'Connor joined us for a drink. Ron asked Kevin to sing us some songs, and he went up on to a little stage to perform. We all had one of the best evenings ever.

Another time we were joined by two little midgets who were friends of Ron's. John Pearson, the author, who wrote a book about us titled *The Profession of Violence*, was in the pub researching for the book. Ron spoke to the two midgets quietly. He said to them, "See that feller over there? He's writing a book on me and Reg, but I want to make sure he doesn't mug us off, so before the night's out, have a word with him and tell him to be careful." I watched all this from a distance, and it was quite amusing. The two midgets walked to the bar where Pearson was standing and they tugged at his trousers. I could see he was already reeling from the number of drinks he'd had. He looked down in startled amazement and the two midgets stared back at him as though looking up at a skyscraper. Before Pearson could recover from his shock, one of the midgets snarled at him while the other one gave another tug at his trouser leg and said, "If you mug the twins off, you'll have us to deal with!" Pearson could only look more amazed, and gulped his G&T down as though in disbelief. He left a little while afterwards.

It was this type of humour which made my nights. Ron and I were in our element, being nocturnal anyway, and I did find it difficult to get used to being locked up at 8 pm or 9 pm in the evenings when I was first sentenced. Even today, over twenty years later, I still get out of bed in the early hours to listen to my radio while having a cup of tea.

Occasionally, I see the past as though it's on film in front of me, and it's always these highlights of humour and good times which stand out more than the bad experiences. It must be that nature made us this way, to remember happiness more than sorrow in the seesaw of life.

It wasn't all a party, though. As I said, a lot of our drinking was for business purposes, and during our reign, up until we got our life sentences, Ron and I had the control of thirty-three clubs throughout London plus many long-term fraud firms, one public house and various other interests. And it was Ron and I who were the instigators of all these businesses. We brought money in legally and otherwise through drinking and gambling clubs, crooked bonds deals, frauds, selling stolen goods, getting fees for looking after businesses, selling phoney jewellery . . . A lot of money was involved, but I haven't a clue how much. Apart from the clubs which we ran, we didn't keep books.

Ron and I and the people who worked for us were known in the East End as "the firm". The role of our workforce was to earn money the best way they could and to be there, present, if violence was necessary.

In the late fifties and sixties, violence of some form or another was sometimes necessary when we were looking after or running clubs. For example, one night Ron and I were sitting in the basement gambling room of a club called The Regency in Stoke Newington. Suppers were always served, and on this particular night, three fellers who had eaten a Chinese meal refused to pay their bill. So I walked over to their table and said politely to the most aggressive of the three, "I take care of any problems here. Are you going to pay the bill or not?"

The loudmouth got even more aggressive and abusive with his language, so I grabbed him with my left hand by the collar and tie, and squeezed hard till he was choking. Then I dropped my left hand and raised it again with a quick left hook to the jaw. The impact had him half KO'd, thick blood came from his mouth and I knew I had broken his jaw. I and a couple of others showed the group to the door. That was almost the end of the matter, but I always took precautions. I knew he'd have to go to the hospital to have his jaw wired up, so I stayed away from the club for more than a week in case the loudmouth made a statement to the police.

A few days later, Ron, Charlie, Freddie Foreman and I were having a cup of tea when Ian Barrie and Scotch Jack Dickson came in to join us. They said the police had been to the Regency making inquiries about a feller who had his jaw broken in the casino. The detective said he would like to find out who did the damage because the surgeon who wired the jaw up stated that the victim had been smashed so hard, it was as though he'd been hit with a sledgehammer. The detective said he would like to shake the hand of anyone who could hit that hard.

I could punch hard with either hand, so much so that I broke eleven jaws that I know of. But, basically, I was a club owner and a good host, and I was in my element when making people happy rather than creating misery.

The people who worked for us were friends of ours. If we liked them and thought we could trust them, they were accepted on to the firm. There was no joining or initiation performance.

You'd hear people saying things like, "Have you seen any of the firm tonight?" or "There's one of the Kray firm over there." If we thought a new feller was capable, we'd say, "You're on the firm now."

So it was no surprise that during our trials at the Old Bailey, the prosecution would leap on to the word "firm", and try to score a point by using it against us. When Ron went into the witness box, he was aware of this, so when he was asked, "Is it right that you and your gang are known as 'the firm'?" he replied, "No." The prosecutor insisted that we were known as "the firm", so then Ron dramatically pulled out a small pocket dictionary from his back trouser pocket and said, "I will look it up." He already had the page creased down, ready, and he held the dictionary out to the prosecutor and said, "Look at this, the word firm means 'commercial enterprise'." Ron went on to say, "Well, I'm out of work and I have not got a factory or any commercial enterprise, so it looks like you're wrong again." This episode brought a little humour into our day in court.

Ron and I were the ones that all the firm answered to, Charlie was in our shadows, and the order of authority then passed from "Scotch" Pat (Pat Connolly), to Big Tommy Brown, who was known as "The Bear", and "Scotch" Ian, although he didn't join us until the mid sixties. Other names springing to mind are Big Albert (Albert Donoghue), Nobby Clarke, Dave Simmonds, Sammy Lederman, Billy Donovan, and many others who came and went over the years.

One member of the firm we could have done without was "Scotch" Jack Dickson. He joined at the same time as "Scotch" Ian, but the difference between them was that Ian was loyal to the end.

"Scotch" Jack had a beetroot red, spongy face. Ron used to have him around as a kind of joker, and sometimes he would bring young fellers into the company, knowing this would please Ron. When I think of all the real villains I've met, I feel disgusted that we had such a creep as Dickson in our company. Some of the tales told to me by his young fellers would make anyone feel embarrassed, and I'm more than broad-minded. It was said during the trial that he was an ex-Royal Marine commando. Yet he couldn't fight his grandmother. A feller we knew called Connie Whitehead nearly knocked Dickson's eye out with a bottle, and he was in hospital for three weeks after this attack.

During our trials, the slag gave evidence against us to save his own skin. My barrister, Paul Wrightson, counted up and listed thirty-three lies in Dickson's evidence. It was farcical. This creep, like others, had the cheek to write a book about us. He is still poncing from the days he lived off us.

Discipline in and outside the firm was enforced by Ron and me by persuasion, reason, and by the fact that we were better at violence than the others were. We had mastered both boxing and street fighting. In boxing, obviously, there are rules and regulations. In street fighting, there are no rules. Anything and everything goes—head butts, kicking, biting, using knees and gouging with the thumb.

But two of my most memorable brushes with the law, back in the early days, were nothing to do with fighting. One of them concerned my late friend Ronnie Marwood who was twenty-three when, one evening, in the area of Finsbury Park, he stabbed a policeman to death. I helped him stow away and looked after him when he was on the run from the police for murder.

At the time, I had the Double R Club, and one day a police chief inspector came into the club and said to me, "49 Lake View Estate." He then walked out of the club. It was his way of telling me that he knew the address of Marwood's hideaway.

I had also visited Marwood in a flat over in West London during the time he was on the run. He had grown a moustache, and had dyed his hair ginger. The flat was full of empty beer crates, and he had the company of an ex-club hostess, but it was obvious that his time on the run was getting on his nerves. He had in his possession a revolver. He showed it to me and said, "I will shoot the bastards if I'm cornered."

Knowing he was armed put me off staying in the hideaway flat with him for too long, because I did not wish to be involved in any shoot-outs. But I stayed long enough to give him a few quid and comfort him before leaving.

One day during this time, the police from Bow Road came to the Double R Club and said they wished to see me at the station. I went along there and was shown into the main interrogation room. I was told by the governor of the station that they knew I had looked after Marwood, so in future the spotlight would be on me wherever I went and in whatever premises I opened as clubs. I expected this as part of my profession, knowing that I was on the other side of the fence, and I would have done it all over again if the same situation occurred, in accordance with the set of rules we lived by.

It has been written in other books that I described Marwood as a small hood and that I regretted protecting him, that I should have handed him over to the law. This is a diabolical lie, and is completely at odds with my whole code of ethics. Marwood, in the end, did not have a shoot-out, but gave himself up. He was hanged in Pentonville Prison. Before the hanging, he and I exchanged letters. I found it a sad and harrowing experience.

My own life was further disrupted by the law in 1959 when I was framed and sentenced to eighteen months for demanding money with menaces.

It all began one day in our billiard hall when a feller called Danny Shay came to see me in his new sports car. He said to me and George Osbourne, another friend of mine, "Do you want to come for a ride to try out the car? I have someone I've got to see over in Finchley Road." I did not particularly fancy going, and my instinct told me not to, but Shay persisted, so I foolishly agreed.

George and I joined Shay in the car. But what he didn't tell us was that he was going to see a Polish feller called Murray Podlo who owed him some money on a gambling debt. Shay pulled the car up outside a leather shop and asked if we would like to come into the shop and look around while he spoke to Podlo. This we did, but after a couple of minutes, an argument started between Podlo and Shay, and it led to a scuffle. So I stepped in and butted Podlo in the face, blacking his eye, before leaving the shop. I don't know why, but I had a bad feeling about this particular day.

Two nights later I was in the Double R Club when three plain-clothes coppers from Finchley Road police station came in and said they wished to speak to me. One of the three, who was called Evans, said I was wanted for demanding money with menaces. I was taken to the station and charged. So were Shay and Osbourne.

When I first went into the leather shop, I had given a Double R Club calling card to Podlo, as I was always looking for new customers, and I told him to call in if he was ever in the East End. This was hardly the act of a criminal who was out to threaten people.

At an earlier hearing in Bow Street Magistrates Court, Podlo said in evidence that I had threatened to cut him up and had demanded the sum of £100. He retracted these lies at the Old Bailey on verbal oath, yet I was still found guilty, even though I proved I had left my calling card and was the owner of four clubs.

For me to threaten to cut someone for a lousy £100 would have been completely out of character. At the time, I was giving this kind of money to my doormen. I would hardly jeopardize my club career to demand money with menaces for such a paltry sum.

My conviction was all over the newspapers, and this was when our reputation for protection rackets began. It's utter rubbish. Ron and I have protected clubs in the past, but only because other people had asked us to do so. *They* requested *our* services for a fee.

At my trial in the Old Bailey, I was prosecuted by Paul Wrightson, QC. Years later, he was to defend me on different charges including my murder case.

On the day of the verdict, I was taken to a cell below the Old Bailey, and sitting in the corner of the same cell was a smartly dressed man of slight build and dark complexion. He had a trilby in his hand, and he greeted me in a friendly manner. I recognized him as Eugene Messina. I did not normally respect ponces, in fact I used to make a target out of them, but with Eugene Messina it was different. He was a man of class and his upbringing and culture did not forbid his way of earning money. His family were Maltese. They were headed by Eugene and Carmello Messina who had come to this country years before and were legendary throughout the London underworld circles, particularly in the area of Mayfair. They successfully ran a multi-million pound organization of high-class prostitution, and lived off immoral earnings. Their operation reached into upper-crust circles, and they occasionally hit the headlines. They were finally exposed by the *People* newspaper reporter Duncan Webb in a series of articles.

Eugene told me in the cells that day that the prostitutes had given perjured evidence against him to gain a conviction. I genuinely believed that he was innocent on this particular charge, even if he was a professional ponce. He received a four-year sentence, and we both went off in the same black maria.

I let it be known in Wandsworth that I objected to some of the lesser slags in the prison having a go at him, because I saw him as a professional, even if I despised his way of earning money. He obviously appreciated my attitude. In the year 1967, he sent an emissary all the way from Malta where he was living in retirement, inviting Ron and me to come and be his guests and talk business with him. We were still considering his proposal when we got arrested the year afterwards, so we will never know what he had in mind.

It is obvious that prison is one place where criminals may meet for the first time and where their paths may cross again in the future. When I was in Wandsworth, I met Jack "The Hat" McVitie for the first time.

A feller called Ray Rosa introduced me, saying, "This is Jack 'The Hat', he's doing seven for robbery." He continued, "He just did that bastard Steinhausen, the Governor of Exeter Prison, and broke his jaw. He's down here for visits." This meant he had come from Exeter to London so that his visitors could come to see him in Wandsworth. Little did I know that years later I would be convicted of the murder of "The Hat". Ironically enough, I, too, would meet Steinhausen—at the start of my life sentence for the killing of Jack McVitie.

Steinhausen became Governor of Leicester Prison where I stayed in the early part of my sentence. The first time I met him in his office, he sarcastically said to me, as though he were Eamonn Andrews, "This is your life, Kray." And he waved his hands in the direction of the small area where I was to live. My mind wandered back to Ray Rosa's words, when he introduced me to McVitie, and I said to myself, "Ray was right, this Steinhausen is a right little bastard." And although I eventually fell out with McVitie, I couldn't help but applaud his attack on Steinhausen, because I felt like doing the same. I learned in later years that my friend Frankie Fraser had also attacked Steinhausen, and Frank was always a good judge of character.

Also in Wandsworth, I met Frank the "Mad Axeman" Mitchell for the first time. He was a prison legend in his own lifetime. Frank had become friends with Ron two years earlier, also in Wandsworth. He had been sentenced to life after escaping from prison while serving a smaller sentence. During the escape, he broke into a house which was occupied by an elderly couple. He threatened them with an axe while robbing the house, but I am sure he would not have carried out the threat, even though he could be very violent.

Frank had a fine physique. He used to work out regularly with expander springs, to develop his chest muscles. He was about five feet eleven and good-looking with strong white teeth. He used to terrify the screws at any prison he was at. He would carry a long knife tucked down his trouser leg, and he did not particularly care if it was seen by the screws. He used to like to taunt them.

One day, we had just left the bath-house and I witnessed Frank go up to a screw, show him the knife, and suggest that the screw should try to take it off him. That was a feat in itself, because the Wandsworth screws were among the roughest in the country.

During his stay at Wandsworth, he stabbed another con in the side, and was charged with attempted murder. His first appearance on this charge was at Bow Street Magistrates Court, and Ron and I had arranged for a well-known woman barrister, Nemone Lethbridge, to defend him. He was acquitted.

We had also arranged, before the trial, to get Frank a suit, shirt, tie, shoes, etc. When I went to see him just after his acquittal, all he wanted to know was if he looked smart in his suit. He asked me repeatedly. It seemed his appearance was more important to him than the court case. He never mentioned the fact that the con he had stabbed was so terrified of reprisals that he had changed his evidence in the courtroom from what was in his original statement.

In later years, I went to see Frank in Durham Prison. He had already been given the cat o' nine tails for attacking screws, and during my visit in a small cubicle, he was surrounded by twelve screws. They took no chances with him.

When he went to Dartmoor, the screws there were terrified of him. He would often grab hold of one and get him in a bear hug. They never knew if he was joking or not. It depended a lot on whether he relaxed his grip or put the pressure on. A couple of screws suffered cracked ribs, but would not report the damage in case Frank got the real needle. The fact that they sacrificed their precious sick pay shows how afraid they were.

Ron and I used to send Frank boxes of old watches and parts. Mending them was his hobby. He liked to tinker with delicate little parts in between putting bear hugs on screws and cracking their ribs. At our 1969 trials, Ron and I were found not guilty of Frank's murder.

But that was ten years away. Back at Wandsworth in 1959, I was making new friends and new discoveries about myself. A padre there gave me one of the best books I have ever read, *Wisdom of the Ages*, which was full of beautiful proverbs. Reading this book stimulated an ambition in me to be a writer.

Ever since I can remember, I have had the inclination to write, and have been particularly interested in the use of the English language, admiring people with the ability to make their speech sound musical. I wrote a story in Wandsworth, compiled in several prison notebooks. It was called *Perez* and was the story of a con in prison who used his influence in the career of a new friend whose ambition was to be a singer. I find it really strange that, some thirty years later, my friend Pete Gillett and I should be the central characters in a true story which so closely reflects the fiction I wrote way back then.

One of my real-life experiences in Wandsworth also inspired me to write. I saw this particular young kid in the prison church just before he was hanged, and his memory stayed with me so strongly that I wrote an essay, in his memory and as an illustration of my stance against capital punishment:

"His name was Flossie Forsyth. He was just turned eighteen years of age and he was due to be hanged by the neck until dead. Young Forsyth had been involved in the killing of another teenager on a towpath in the Peckham area of South London. He had been convicted of murder.

"I could see his shape behind the thick red curtain that covered the cubicle in the right hand corner of the church, close to the altar. I had read the kid's case and seen his photo in the daily newspapers: it was the face of a good-looking, blond-haired boy. Now, as I sat, deep in thought about his terrible plight, I felt great pity. His young life was to be snuffed out like the flickering flame of a candle in just a few days' time.

"I tried to picture his last few days alone in the presence of a group of warders who would watch his every move. They would make sure he would not take his own life. He would have no privacy at all, not even to go through his daily ablutions. I doubt if he would get any last urges to mastur-bate, or to think sexual thoughts. The occasional cold stares of the warders would stifle such thoughts or urges in his discomfort and misery. What comfort could he expect from people so cold and distant, even if one or two of those did try to be friendly in the role of custodian?

"I guess the tears would fall. After all, he was just a boy. Even a man would shed tears, knowing there was no hope. The prison padre would probably visit him to offer some solace and words of advice on how Flossie should be brave in the face of his coming death.

"Everyone wanted things to go smoothly on the day. No fuss or kicking or screams of terror were wanted. The padre, too, was a total stranger, as were the warders. I guess Flossie would yearn for the warm closeness of his parents' household and remember how he would get ready to go out with his mates each night to have some fun.

"It was just one of those kind of nights that led to his present predicament, this nightmare. He and his mates had gone out and had met another kid on the towpath on their way to a local dance hall. Remarks were exchanged between Flossie's group and the other kid. A fight started and all joined in because the lone teenager had put up such a fight. This same boy fell to the path where he lay to die. Forsyth and his friends were eventually arrested and charged with murder; the case was named the 'Towpath Murder'.

"I thought of the victim, too, and it distressed me that a young life should have been taken. To me, they were all victims, there were no victors. I felt sure none of them foresaw the tragedy which would follow in the wake of their night out. I also thought of the parents of each side, and felt great sympathy. I felt like rising from my seat to go to the pulpit and to say aloud: 'Let this kid come with me. I will take care of him. Give him a chance. He is just a teenager. I will straighten him out.'

"He is not an evil person or a killer in the true sense of the word. Fights and attacks were common in the Peckham area at this time. This must have weighed heavily against the accused, been a deciding factor of guilt by association to such an area.

"All these years later, I still think of Forsyth and the haunting sight of this slightly-built figure in the box-like cubicle, and of his last thoughts. I could not fathom how anyone could place a rope around such a young neck and kill like the killing of a chicken. Why could not justice have been tempered with mercy in the case of one so young? One life lost on the towpath was one too many. The death of Forsyth would not act as a deterrent.

"His death was retribution because there was a lack of compassion, understanding and any wish to straighten out a young life. We should try to learn and understand as well as judge and condemn. We should look at the causes and effect. Would one stamp on a flower if it began to wilt? Young Forsyth's life was wasted. He became a statistic when he could have been saved. Were we not all guilty that, in our ignorance, society had not yet learned better than to resort to a rope?

"My brother Ron and I were spared this spectacle. I guess there were those who were disappointed that Ron and I were not to be debased by the ritual of the rope, but I believe that our lives were better for the saving.

"Above all, let us remember the last hours of Flossie Forsyth. In the cold light of day, he would have been woken from his restless sleep and the warmth of the grey prison blankets where he lay curled, as though seeking the sanctuary of his mother's womb once again. He would then have been offered the pleasure of his last request: the choice of meal for breakfast.

"The anxiety would by this time have built up the bile in his queasy stomach, so much so that he would feel physically sick and wish to vomit, and because he had not eaten, his stomach would have been too empty to bring anything up.

"He would have felt panic as the warders closed in on him to escort him on his last few steps on shaky legs. He would have felt faint, too confused to think his last thoughts. He would have felt the coarse thick rope around his neck . . .

"Lest we forget . . ."

CHAPTER 4

OF LOVE AND WAR

I was released from Wandsworth Prison at the dawning of the most exciting decade London has ever known: the sixties. It was an era like a vein of gold in a rich, untapped mine. The music was the greatest, the economy was booming, the city was alive with activity, our club empire was expanding into the West End, and I was in love.

Her name was Frances Shea, she lived in Bethnal Green and she was just a teenager. I met her through her brother Frank, who was a friend of mine, and asked her to come out with me. Soon, we were courting.

Some of my fondest memories are of the nights I would take Frances to the cinemas in the West End of London. We would go to the Odeon in Marble Arch and in the darkness, once we were seated, I would glance round at Frances who had the most beautiful brown eyes I have ever seen, and Frances would know I was looking at her, and she would smile as though pleased. Little things like this are what true love is really all about, the secret type of incidents that make one's heart sing.

I suppose that true love is God's gift of joy. It has no boundaries, and there are no barriers of time or distance. Sometimes, from a long way away, we can see the loved one that much more clearly, as though looking at the outline of a great mountain from far away.

It's said that love and hate walk hand in hand—so many people I meet have both words tattooed on their bodies—but although the intensity of the two emotions can be similar, there is so much difference. Hate can turn inwards and poison the body. Love is for sharing and looking forward.

Frances and I used to sit in the car, parked in a back street of the East End, talking until the early hours, and we would dream together. I would say, "Yes, Frances, we'll travel the world together, and we'll bring back a souvenir from everywhere we go to keep in our mansion." Frances would smile, and her eyes would light up in the darkness as we would go from one dream to another.

I had a plan and a goal to reach for both of us, to take us to the heights, to take us out of the dimly lit streets for a while to where the lights would glitter in Paris, Barcelona or Milan.

Only by sharing can we truly enjoy life. Every couple will know the good feelings of planning a future, of looking forward to the pot of gold at the end of the rainbow with a smile and a twinkle in the eye. What a nice feeling when your girlfriend says to you, "Will we really do all you say?" And you reply, "Of course we will," and she gives you a little kiss of congratulation, and you say to yourself, "Yes, I will reach the target for *us*."

But, alas, as the years go by, we no longer reach out, we put on our carpet slippers and we get old, the rot and the decay set in, because we forget to dream, or because we no longer have the incentive to dream after seeing our previous hopes destroyed. I would never have a pair of bedroom slippers for that reason. All these years later, I'm still a dreamer, and even though Frances is no longer with me, I carry on our dreams for both of us in my own way.

George Raft once told me that the reason he remained young in spirit was that he socialized every night with all kinds of people rather than stay at home. I know that he remained a dreamer, and he lived until the age of eighty-three.

Let's dream and set the world alight, and let's keep it burning!

Ideas are the things that generate the actions that build empires
and scale mountains. Man would not have gone to the moon if
it were not for the dreamers. Columbus would not have set out
on his journey.

The philosophy of the following verses more or less sums it
up for me:

> I bargained with life for a penny,
> And life would pay no more
> However I begged at evening
> When I counted my scanty score.
>
> For life is a just employer,
> He gives you what you ask.
> But once you have set the wages,
> Why, you must bear the task.
>
> I worked for a menial's hire
> Only to learn, dismayed,
> That any wage I had asked of life,
> Life would have willingly paid.

My parents both loved Frances, and when my dad had had a
few drinks, he would say to her, "You would be my kind of girl
if I was Reggie's age again," and Frances would smile.

My mother would glance over from time to time, when we
would all be sitting together in Vallance Road, and say, "Are
you OK, Frances?", just making sure she felt at home.

My parents were always very understanding. When Ron and
I were out working day and night, they never complained, and
still made sure we had a meal in front of us when we needed
one. My mother always had faith in Ron and me, and years
later when we opened our clubs she was very proud of us. She
would say, "I knew you would make it one day."

Both of my parents would come to all our clubs. During the
Double R days and later at our Kentucky Club, my mother
would occasionally sing a few songs through the microphone on

78

the little stage, with the group in the background. She would favour Al Jolson songs like *Sonny Boy* and *Mammy*. Sometimes after the club closed, we would go back to Vallance Road in an untidy convoy of cars and have a private party in the house.

Today, it seems very difficult for me to comprehend that these days ever took place in my lifetime, and when I hear my mother's favourite songs on the radio, I like to think that as the song says, we'll all meet again whenever the time comes for me to depart from this earth, too.

Whenever Ron and I got an extra few quid, we would call my mother into the front room at Vallance Road and start to cut up the money into different piles. We would say, "That's yours, Mum." And she would say, "Ooh, that's nice," and I'd give her another little pile and tell her to give it to Rosy, who helped my mother do the housework. She was a lifelong friend. And we would say, "There's some for the old man, too, but don't give it to him all at once, because he'll only spend it on drink." When we would see Rosy later on, passing through the house, she would say, "Thanks, Reg, Ron," and there would be a warm feeling of camaraderie all around.

We used to have some good times in Vallance Road. I remember the boy who Ron dressed up as a lord as a practical joke on the old man. The boy was called Bob Buckley and he used to speak in a very posh accent. Ron met him in Chelsea, and took him over to Vallance Road. He showed the boy to the upstairs living room and told him to wait there. He then went downstairs where he saw our dad.

He told the old man that he had brought a young lord to see him, and so Dad should smarten himself up, have a shave and put on a shirt and tie. The old man said, "Who is this lord?" Ron told him his name was Lord Buckley. Dad said, "Who the fucking hell are you going to bring home next? Last week it was two midgets, and this week it's a fucking lord."

Ron went upstairs and told Bobby Buckley to play up to the old man that he was a lord. Then he took him downstairs and introduced him as Lord Buckley. My father said, "How are you, M'Lord?" Some weeks later, he found out it was a hoax . . .

Ron has always enjoyed aliases and disguises, ever since he was on the run from Long Grove Hospital and went out in the street wearing bandages around his head, smeared with tomato sauce, so as not to be recognized. But, to Ron's disappointment, the first friend he met knew him straight away!

Then there was the night that Ron wanted a friend of ours to pretend to be an African prince. This was a West African feller called Cha Cha who used to be with us. He was a big, strong man with a huge neck and shoulders. Ron invited him to go to a club on this particular occasion, and he took him to a tailor shop first to fit him out with a dinner jacket and bow tie. Ron said, "We're going to the Society Club in Jermyn Street. Don't say anything while we're there, because I'm going to try and con some money off someone. Just make out you're an African prince."

They went to the Society Club and were sitting at the table with the feller Ron was doing the business with. The waiter came up to the table, and Cha Cha heard Ron order a prawn cocktail. The waiter then asked them what they'd like to drink. Cha Cha said, "I'll have a prawn cocktail, too . . ." He made the pair of them look like fools, and really ruined that piece of business.

He was very loyal to us, Cha Cha. When we were arrested for the murders, the police questioned him for hours, but he made out he was mad and wouldn't answer any questions. They had to let him go in the end. When he died, his coffin was flown back to West Africa.

I've always admired Ron's sense of humour. Sometimes it's unintentional. Some years ago, on one of my periodic visits to see him in Broadmoor, I told him that I'd sent a copy of my book of Cockney expressions, *Slang*, to President Reagan. Ron replied, in all seriousness, "Oh, really. What did he think of it?"

Ron's bisexuality has been a regular talking point over the years. If anyone asks him about it now, he just tells them, "It's nobody else's business. I'm bisexual, that's all. It's now a permissive society. It's old-fashioned, people objecting to others being bisexual."

I remember one of Ron's girlfriends, a girl called Monica. He took her out for about two years, but she eventually married someone else. He still thinks of her as "one of the two most beautiful girls I ever met in my life". The other is a young student who used to visit his best friend Charlie Smith in Broadmoor. Of course, he's happily married now to his wife Kate.

Quite often, I hear about tough-guy cons intimidating gay prisoners who are nice fellers but not fighting men. This type of bullying I despise. It seems to give these ignorant, bigoted people a feeling of macho power. I have seen these same loud-mouthed cons, who seem to think they're judges with their moralizing and so-called principles, going from cell to cell in search of the most vile and depraved types of magazines they can find to satisfy their filthy, lustful desires. What they read, I see as their reference. I see them for what they are—hypocrites, casting stones at others and forgetting they live in a glass house.

Some time ago, a story in a tabloid newspaper stated that there was a gay relationship between me and my friend Peter Gillett while we were doing time together in Parkhurst. This was a pack of lies, but if it had been true, I would not have been ashamed to say so. I see no reason to knock gay people, either inside prison, where many men are serving long-term sentences, or outside it. I have known gay people who are tougher than all the bullies who run round picking on the weak, some of them world-class champions of the ring, racing drivers and villains, including Mafia men.

There's one villain from South London who could knock most adversaries out with one punch, and if he was in a real bad mood, would cut an enemy so badly he would need a new face. Another villain from Paddington was so feared that even troublemakers would stay away from him. Both of these men were bisexual.

The great fighter Emile Griffith killed Benny Paret in their world title bout because Paret called him a "queer". And one of George Cornell's many mistakes was to make derogatory remarks about Ron in public.

But George Cornell was the least of our worries in the early sixties. We were busy adding to our string of clubs and, unsurprisingly, having the occasional run-in with the law. In 1961, Ron was acquitted of trying car doors in a street in Dalston, and I was found not guilty of robbing a flat. By then, our activities were a lot more ambitious than that.

We opened two new clubs within months of each other. The first was the Kentucky Club in Mile End Road in the summer of 1962, and the second was Esmerelda's Barn, which included a twisting club, a lesbian club and a gambling floor, in Wilton Place, Knightsbridge. This quickly turned into one of the best and most profitable clubs of its kind in London.

Eric Clapton, the legendary guitarist, played some of the earliest shows of his career at the Barn. Our manager there was a feller called Laurie O'Leary, and his brother Alfie ended up taking a job with Clapton's entourage and travelling all over the world with him. I followed Eric Clapton's career with interest, and his LP *Slowhand* has remained amongst my favourites.

The Walker Brothers—whose record *The Sun Ain't Gonna Shine Any More* was playing on the jukebox when Ron shot George Cornell—also appeared at Esmerelda's Barn.

These are just a couple of famous names among many who came to our clubs to perform or to enjoy a night out. At the Kentucky Club, we hosted a party for the cast of the Barbara Windsor film *Sparrers Can't Sing* on the night of its royal première.

It was also at the beginning of the sixties that we began to realize how much money it was possible to raise for charity. In 1961, we had our first involvement with the Mayor of Bethnal Green's Old People Appeal, via the Repton Tournament, and we held regular fund-raising nights at the Kentucky and other clubs.

The most unusual of these was in 1963. I was on holiday in the South of France, and I phoned Ron in London to see how things were going. Ron said, "Well, I've earned a few quid, so we'll cut it up when you get back." I returned to Vallance Road and Ron produced the money, but it was over £500 short, which was a lot in those days. Ron said, "I spent it on a racehorse for the old lady." Ron and I always referred to our mother as the old lady. The horse's name was Solway Cross and it was being trained at Epsom. It was eventually entered in a race, but it came last, so Ron decided to put it up for raffle in aid of charity at our club/restaurant, the Cambridge Rooms, Kingston Bypass.

The horse was placed in a large white marquee, next door to the restaurant. We had laid down imitation green turf, which made a beautiful setting for the animal, and there was a buffet on offer there, too. The raffle was attended by various celebrities including Barbara Windsor, Lenny Peters, the jazz singer Lita Roza, and Ron Frazer, the actor. The horse was won by Ron Frazer, but he was drunk at the time. So he woke up the next day with a racehorse, not knowing what to do with it. That was the last we saw of Solway Cross.

I have had many pets over the years, and so has Ron. My favourite was Mitzi, a beautiful Pekinese dog which was like a human being. I would say to her, "Get your lead, we're going over the park," and she would pick up the lead and run to the end of the passage, planting her paws on the street door until I opened it. Then, Mitzi would rush to my car which was outside and would get in and leap up to the back window. We would walk over Victoria Park for an hour or more, and when I would say, "Home, Mitzi," she would rush back to the car and up to the window again. Mitzi would also roll over on to her back and play dead if I pointed my fingers at her like a gun. One time when I hadn't seen her for three months, because I was on remand in Brixton Prison, she leaped up into my arms on my arrival back at Vallance Road, and would not stop licking my face for over half an hour.

Sadly, she got run over and killed at the caravan site we stayed on near Southend. The sad death of this beautiful little dog brought tears to my eyes. I buried her near my caravan and planted a rose tree in the soil above her.

Ron was always buying pedigree dogs, and he sent one, a bull terrier puppy, to New York by plane as a present for the children of Eddie Pucci. Eddie Pucci, in later years, was shot to death on a golf course by Mafia hitmen.

As is well known, Ron also bought a donkey which he would bring into the Kentucky club, where Tex the midget would sit on its back and play the guitar. I also had a donkey which I named Figaro. I kept it on the acres of land which adjoined the mansion we bought in Bildeston further on in our career. All the local kids would take rides on it.

Other famous Kray-zee pets were the two snakes Ron bought from Harrods, boas which he kept in a glass case and called Gerrard and Read, the names of the two coppers who were always after us. They had to be fed on live mice, which wasn't very nice to watch because they would crush and swallow the mice whole. We knew our phones were tapped, so Ron would say to any of the firm who rang, "I'm just going to feed Gerrard and Read again," and he would laugh aloud.

We had animals around from the earliest age. I remember the black, shiny mongrel dog we had at Vallance Road. When he was not playing with us, he would roam the streets, sow his seeds and enjoy himself in general. In my opinion, there is no more loyal and affectionate friend than a dog.

Certainly, there was very little loyalty and affection from the firm we built around us, as was proved at our 1969 trials when all of them, with a few exceptions, turned Judas. On reflection, it would have been better for Ron and me to work alone, because we didn't need anyone else. All we did was keep a lot of dead bodies in spending money.

In the early sixties, though, we didn't anticipate any such problems. Life was good, we had friends around us, or so we thought, our clubs were doing well, and we were out and about expanding our list of business interests and contacts—and coming across the usual assortment of characters.

Anyone who was around at that time will remember the name of Peter Rachman whose activities made such a mark that "Rachmanism" became an established word in the English language. He was about five feet ten in height and of burly build with a protruding stomach. Both he and his partner Raymond Nash were always smartly dressed and wore large dark glasses. I would often see Rachman going into the Odeon, Leicester Square, always with a beautiful blonde on his arm. I believe I'm right in saying he was Polish.

He and Raymond Nash earned a fortune by letting out near-derelict premises for high rents, mainly in the Bayswater and Paddington areas of London. The term "Rachmanism" was created during a debate in the House of Commons when a question about this rent racketeering was tabled in motion.

On another occasion, the national newspapers blasted the Lebanese Raymond Nash for running a seedy dance hall establishment in Wardour Street in the West End. In this particular place, couples would be seen kissing and cuddling on mattresses in the four corners of the large room, and it was said that one could freely buy pep pills. While the music was playing, Raymond Nash would sit on a chair on the stage playing bongo drums. He was a good-looking, well-built feller, and was a black belt at Judo.

It was after the newspapers exposed his drinking club/dance hall, and also because he had something to do with the anti-establishment newspaper *Private Eye*, that he was slung out of the country, but just before his dismissal, he and Rachman contacted Ron and me and asked to see us. We arranged to meet them at the Regency Club in Stoke Newington.

Ron and I brought along three others for this meet. Rachman and Nash arrived on time and the five of us sat at a table near the bar. While we were being served drinks, we listened to the proposition. Rachman and Nash wanted to give us £500 a month to let them use our name while collecting their rents. They figured the name of the Krays would save them paying out as much again to hire muscle, and that they would get better results, too. We listened intently and considered the proposal, but we turned it down because we didn't want to get involved in that kind of business.

Some time after Nash was forced to go back to the Lebanon,

Peter Rachman died of heart trouble at an early age. Great mystery and speculation surrounded his death. It was said at the time that the body they buried was not that of Peter Rachman but of a large, overweight tramp. The rumour went that Rachman owed so much in back taxes, he wished to disappear to evade payment and prosecution. I doubt myself if there was any substance to this story. Rachman had the brains to get out of the situation if he did owe taxes. He was also grossly overweight, and his sex orgies were legend, so there was every probability he had a heart attack as a result of his way of life.

Around the same time we came across Charles De Silva, the king of the conmen, through an introduction by Billy Hill. A bully by the name of Charlie Mitchell was taking liberties with De Silva, taking money off him whenever he conned anyone. Billy Hill said to Ron and me that if Charles De Silva was going to give money to that slag Mitchell, we may as well put ourselves on Charles's firm and row Mitchell out.

Ron and I met De Silva at the Star public house in Belgravia, Knightsbridge. He looked just like Omar Sharif, the actor. He was Ceylonese by birth, and was the black sheep of a very rich family. He lived like a king, stayed in all the best hotels in Europe, liked fast cars, good clothes, fine food and wine, and loved beautiful women.

He agreed that we should look after him because, being a top conman, he was vulnerable to reprisals and also to villains who wanted some of his easy pickings. He was staying in the largest suite in the Mayfair Hotel in Park Lane, booked for three months. All the staff were under the impression he was a sheikh, and the waitresses hovered around him like flies, since he was very generous with his tips.

On the day we met him there, he wore an immaculate dark suit. He had at one time served a seven-year sentence at Parkhurst Prison, because one of his gigantic frauds had been discovered by the law. He had vowed never to go back to prison again. He was not cut out for the coarse clothing, or for prison life. He found most of the cons ignorant and insensitive. He was used to only the best, as someone who had amassed a fortune over the years through his various guises and deceptions. But the fact that he liked classy living sent that fortune slipping through his hands, and he always had to get involved in another high-finance con. He was also one of the top gamblers in London. We saw him win or lose fortunes without batting an eyelid.

The last of his great cons was when he found a sucker of a farmer and sold him a fishing fleet which did not exist for an enormous amount of money. But while De Silva was having a good time spending it, the law tracked him down and arrested him. He managed to get bail, tidied up his affairs and took his life with a large overdose of drugs. He knew he would get at least another seven years, and he preferred to end his days outside the prison, rather than spend them inside it.

Another of the more unlikely criminals we encountered at that time was "Playboy" Peter Jenkins. He had, in his teens, been to one of England's top upper-class schools, and had gone on to college. But in his twenties, he developed such a great thirst for high living and spending money that he and one of his friends, who was also an ex-public schoolboy, decided to take to crime. Jenkins, like De Silva, lived extravagantly and was always to be seen in exclusive, high-society establishments. He had the charm and manners to be the centre of attention wherever he was.

In his first and only crime, he and his partner decided they would try to steal a valuable tray of rings and diamonds, so they booked in at one of London's top hotels and phoned through to a jeweller they had already visited, inviting him to the hotel with the tray.

As he approached the hotel, the jeweller was struck down by Jenkins and his colleague, who were wielding coshes. They escaped capture for a time because they were not men with convictions, but somehow they were eventually found and arrested. This caused a sensation in society circles, and during their trial, the public gallery was packed out with beautiful debutantes. Jenkins received seven years, and would have got longer if he had not been of previous good character.

He was sent to Wandsworth to start his sentence and then to Dartmoor which at the time housed the most dangerous prisoners in England. This new prison society was repugnant to him, but he was a likeable enough person to be accepted by the criminal element as one of their own. Hadn't he coshed the jeweller? Yes, they agreed, he was one of the chaps. Ron and I also started to count Jenkins as one of those we looked after and sent Christmas cards to each year.

When he was released, we invited him to the Double R Club for a drink and, of course, we gave him a few quid, as was the custom in those days. He seemed to me to be a person out of his natural environment. I could see that the sentence had destroyed him; he seemed to lack confidence, and did not appear to be sure of his own direction. I believe he felt that his public schoolboy background was not such a great asset in the world of the criminal where people are successful just by being streetwise. But at the same time, the people in the society he truly belonged to shunned him like a leper, and he went steadily downhill.

Eventually, the police found his unkempt body in a dingy flat in Bayswater amongst the empty Scotch bottles and the cigarette butts littered all over the floor. Just middle-aged, he died, an alcoholic, due to kidney trouble.

Indeed, the Double R Club saw many interesting and infamous characters within its walls, and if there are ghosts of the past, its ghosts are the ones who tried, at least, to make the best of life while they could.

Ron and I, meanwhile, were trying to make the best of our opportunities by investing abroad. We became aware of a proposed development project in a town called Enugu, the capital of Eastern Nigeria. Ernest Shinwell, the son of Labour MP Manny Shinwell, wanted to build a housing estate and factories there, and he invited us to come in on it. We discussed this idea with Leslie Payne, a former businessman who had been working with us since the beginning of the sixties. We held negotiations over the plan throughout 1963 and we both visited Enugu. On one occasion, Ron went there with Ernest Shinwell who asked him if there was anything he would like to see or do. Ron said he would like to go to a tribal dance, which was duly arranged. He was given refreshments of monkey meat and palm wine while he watched the children dancing with bells round their ankles, and the grown men with their spears.

We were treated like dignitaries in Enugu. We would be greeted by the Prime Minister of the region, Dr M. I. Okpara, and the Minister of Health, Chief B. C. Okwu. There would be a police escort into Enugu, and great hospitality on arrival.

On another occasion, Ron was again asked if he wished to be taken anywhere in particular, and he told them he would very much like to visit the local prison. He was taken on this tour in an official capacity, telling his hosts that he had an interest in criminology. His only comment about the jail was that "I couldn't get out of there fast enough", although he did stay for a few extra moments to have his picture taken with a Nigerian warder outside the gates. I still have the photograph. Needless to say, both Ron and I have since lost our interest in criminology . . .

We went to Enugu twice on business trips to do with the housing project, and Les Payne and our brother Charlie also made a visit there on their own. That's when Ron and I saved their lives.

Luckily for them, we were at our mother's house in Vallance Road when the Nigerian Commissioner phoned and told us that he had placed Les Payne in the prison. He had confiscated Charlie's passport and ordered him to stay in house custody in their hotel near the airport. We were told that if we did not place £5,000 into the Nigerian bank near the City of London within twenty-four hours, Charlie would be put into the prison, too, where he would remain with Payne for an indefinite period.

The Commissioner claimed that they were responsible for defrauding by deception a Nigerian businessman out of £5,000.

I should point out that Nigerian prisons have much more meagre food rations than we do here. They are also filthy. A European in prison in Nigeria would be open to malaria, dysentery, and countless other diseases, and there's always the possibility of death by malnutrition. The European would not be so hardy as the Nigerian prisoner.

Ron and I informed Les Payne's wife and Charlie's wife Dolly that their husbands were in dire straits. We also asked both ladies if they would put up the £5,000 needed by the Nigerian bank, or at least something towards it. Both claimed they were poverty-stricken, as Ron and I had foreseen. They probably went right off to the hairdresser's to have a good natter about it.

Ron and I raised the £5,000 within twenty-four hours and placed it in the bank. Charlie and Payne returned to England. Ron and I watched with amusement the crocodile tears of Lady Kray and Lady Payne. They would have left Elizabeth Taylor and Joan Collins standing in the Academy Awards. I also noted the various pieces of jewellery dangling all over these ladies, yet not one piece was offered towards the cost of saving their husbands in an hour of need.

A lot has been said about the so-called brains of the firm, Les Payne. He was another who had to get his wife's permission to stay out late. He was not the brains he was said to have been. Ron and I just saw him as a good front man, because he had no criminal convictions. As I said before, it was Ron and I who made all the connections.

At one point, we approached the Tory MP Lord Boothby about a potential collaboration on the Enugu project, but he couldn't help. A couple of innocent meetings with him, at which photos were taken, led to a scandal in the press, alleging that he was having an affair with Ron. One headline screamed: "The Peer And The Gangster." Although Ron and Boothby did become friends, this was a ridiculous accusation, and Lord Boothby received £40,000 damages in 1964 from the *Sunday Mirror*.

Also in 1964, it became apparent that something was going wrong with the project. Shinwell started getting into difficulty, and Payne appealed to a feller called Hew McCowan, the son of a rich baronet, for more backing money. But the project was already on the verge of collapse. Ron and I had put thousands of pounds into it, and we lost the lot because of the incompetence of those who were dealing with things on our behalf. Today, Ron still blames Payne for "messing it all up because he never had any brains". We realized that too late.

During our trials, Les Payne was a major prosecution witness, one of the first to rush to make a statement against us in return for an agreement that the police would save his skin. On reflection, I think we should have left him in the Nigerian jail.

It was also in 1964 that Ron and I rented on lease two luxury flats at Cedra Court in Cazenove Road, Clapton. I had the ground-floor flat and Ron had the one above it. The rent was £10 a week. I went to stores in Ilford to buy all the furniture for my flat. I had a good idea myself how the décor should look, but I called in a specialist to fix the curtains and pelmet.

The bathroom and toilet were all pink enamel, and I even had pink-coloured mirrors put in there. I also arranged for a different colour of telephone to be put into each room, matching the décor. There was a spyhole in the door so I could see who was ringing the bell.

Ron also had a security spyhole, and he had a massive tropical fish tank in one of his rooms. In the bedroom, he had a huge four-poster bed.

In those days, I also had a 220 SE Mercedes with the unusual number of B77, so we were living in style.

Around the same time, I had slashed the face of a villain by the name of Bulla Ward. He had about ninety stitches put in and, years later, at Parkhurst, he wrote a book telling how he had planned revenge on me. He said he intended to sling a bomb through my flat window at Cedra Court, and, another time, how he decided to run me over as I stood outside the Green Dragon gambling club in Whitechapel. I had already had wire mesh put round the window frames of my flat because I considered the ground-floor bedroom window was a danger. Ward's book proved me right.

Our clubs were continuing to thrive. Sometimes there would be minor disturbances in the lesbian club at Esmerelda's Barn, which was named the Cellar Club, but otherwise, everyone in the three parts of the building could be assured of a good night which would go on until the early hours. Contrary to what has been written in various books, I would like to make it clear that it was Ron and I who acquired Esmerelda's Barn, no matter what other partners we might have had. Ron and I could always pack or empty a club depending on what our wishes were. Lord Effingham was one of our directors at the Barn, and Commander Diamond and many other members of the establishment were patrons.

By this time, thanks to Ron's efforts, we were also partners to the Green Dragon club and another nearby, also in Whitechapel, called Dodgers.

Judy Garland was our guest at the Crown pub in Cheshire Street, Bethnal Green, that year, and we were pleased to welcome our friend Joe Louis, the great fighter, to England. He flew in for a cabaret engagement at the Newcastle club La Dolce Vita.

But although it had been a good year, there was trouble in store in its closing weeks. By January 1965, Ron and I were in the cells in Brixton Prison awaiting trial. We were charged that between October 1964 and the New Year, we had demanded money with menaces from Hew McCowan.

We had first come into contact with McCowan when Leslie Payne asked him for money to put into the Enugu project. Now, it was being said that we had demanded money from his profits at the Hideaway Club which he ran in Gerrard Street, Soho. Ron was also charged with possession of a knife.

Five weeks later we were still on remand, with no chance of bail, and this situation led to Lord Boothby asking in Parliament how this could be, and on what grounds we were being refused bail.

The trial finally took place in March, but the jury failed to agree and a retrial was ordered. QC Paul Wrightson, who in the past had worked for the prosecution against me, was now defending me, and on 5 April we were cleared of the charges by an Old Bailey jury. We went straight home to Vallance Road to celebrate with our family. We received a cable of congratulations from Judy

Garland. And Frances and I decided to get married as soon as possible.

At the end of those trials, it was suggested that we had got at the jury so as to get an acquittal. Well, let's imagine that a man found himself in the dock when totally innocent, discovered that perjured evidence was being used against him by the police, and realized that the only way out was for him to corrupt a jury. Would he do so through his friends, or would he suffer the consequences of a long jail sentence passed on him because of fabricated evidence?

On more than one occasion when I've found myself faced with this moral dilemma, I've acted in accordance with the will to survive, and so did corrupt some members of a particular jury. I have known this to happen in many criminal trials over the years, where friends of mine had been fitted up by the police.

Ask yourself: what would you do if you had the means to corrupt and sway the jury and walk to freedom, when you knew you should not have even been in the dock in the first place? Crooked police officers, namely detectives, are treacherous. Most uniformed police are bona fide.

The legal costs before my acquittal were so vast that I had to lose my luxury flat, a cottage and 600 acres of land on the tip of Bantry Bay in Ireland, due to being fitted up on a demanding charge. It is when you lose such property, and stand to lose your freedom for a long time, that one has to evaluate the pros and cons of that one course of action. Should one tamper with a jury? My answer was, yes. Where crooked police are concerned, who corrupt the system by using crooked evidence to gain a conviction, I would always say fight fire with fire, and let God above decide who was meant for heaven and hell.

As a result of some of my acquittals, the jury system was changed to that which is in practice today, with verdicts decided by a majority. Before, one juror's disagreement would mean a retrial.

Meanwhile, in an ironic postscript to the court case, Ron and

93

I took over the Hideaway Club almost immediately and renamed it El Morocco.

On 19 April 1965, I married Frances, who was twenty-one. I chose to walk to the church rather than be driven in the blue Bentley which was at my disposal. I wanted to take in the full feeling of the day. When I got to St James' Church, Bethnal Green, I could not help but notice that my mother-in-law was dressed in black, like some Sicilian *Mafiosa*. But the sight of my mother dressed all in white, with a nice white hat, too, outweighed this darkness. Frances was a beautiful young bride, and I felt a bit intoxicated throughout the whole day—not just because I had a couple of gin and tonics either, but they did help!

It was a big day in the Bethnal Green social calendar. Ron was the best man, David Bailey took the wedding photos, and some of our favourite boxing and entertainment celebrities mingled as guests among our families and friends.

I enjoyed the ride with Frances in the Bentley to London Airport where we caught a plane to Athens in Greece. But after a wonderful honeymoon, we returned to England to discover, to our sadness, that ours was not to be a happy marriage. This may seem strange, because we had all the ingredients for a good life together. Financially we were OK, we had moved into a lovely luxury flat and we had a lively social life, going to exclusive clubs, show-business parties, and fine restaurants. But Frances was caught up in an agonizing tug-of-love between her parents and me. Mr and Mrs Shea had disapproved of me from the beginning, I had never felt comfortable in their home, and they were no happier about my relationship with Frances after our wedding, despite the fact that I gave her father, whose name, like her brother's, was Frank, a job in one of our clubs. I did try to make our marriage happy, but circumstances dictated that I was to fail.

By the end of the year we had separated, and although we saw each other nearly every day, Frances continued to stay with her family. The strain of the situation, with her parents trying to keep her away from me, made her ill. She suffered a breakdown and, on two occasions, she attempted to commit suicide.

As has been widely reported, her mother announced, untruthfully, that the marriage was not consummated in a bid to have it annulled. At the same time, coincidentally, a woman called Anna Zambodini issued a paternity claim against me, alleging I was the father of her baby daughter. Just as I knew it would be, the case was dismissed.

In 1966, it became obvious that I would never have Frances back with me again. I still loved her deeply, but the opposition of her parents made any long-lasting reconciliation impossible. Life had to go on, and in March of that year, events took their most dramatic turn yet.

George Cornell came from Watney Street in East London. Ron and I had known him during our early twenties. We were all friendly, but not what you'd call close friends. Ron had helped Cornell when he first came out of prison after serving a four-year sentence. Ron had got him fitted up with clothes, and put him on a pension for a time. This few quid had helped George settle back into society again.

But then, some time later, George moved across to the South London area. Many of us in the East End did not like the way this seemed to change him. He started to associate with Charlie and Eddie Richardson, "Mad" Frankie Fraser and their firm, south of the river. He appeared to be looking down upon his old friends, and this was when the rift between Ron and me and Cornell really began.

Cornell was of a violent disposition. He had convictions for various crimes, including three years for slashing the face of a woman garage attendant. He was about five feet eight and a half tall, with fair hair, a reasonably good-looking, but stern, face and a thick neck. He had an older brother called Jimmy who had a bad scar down the right side of his face where someone had slashed him with a knife. Jimmy and George had both been dockers.

In 1964, Cornell made the first of the bad mistakes that were to lead to his death. While Ron and I were on remand in

Brixton on the "money with menaces" charge, Cornell told Dave Simmonds, who was one of our firm, that "the king is dead". This was an insulting reference to Ron which was his wishful thinking. Cornell, in effect, was saying that he hoped Ron would get convicted. When we were released from Brixton, Ron heard about this from Dave Simmonds, and made a mental note.

To make matters worse, a young feller, who was a good friend of Ron's, was at a party in a house in South London one night, when Cornell made insulting remarks to him about Ron. One was that Ron was a "poof". Ron hated this word, and he made another note in the back of his mind. Cornell would not say any of these things to Ron's face, because he knew Ron would hit him on the chin.

At this particular time, too, Cornell was also torturing people he had the needle with. He was pulling their teeth out with pliers, and giving electric shocks to their testicles. Some of our distant friends were caught up in the wild frenzy of Cornell's ruthlessness. Add this to the jibes and taunts Cornell had uttered, and it's not surprising that Ron took an intense dislike to him.

Ron had been thinking for some time of some form of revenge to even the score. Then came the news that George Cornell was involved in the death of Dickie Hart, who was a friend of ours, during gang warfare with guns at a club called Mr Smith's in Catford, early in March 1966.

Charlie and Eddie Richardson and Frankie Fraser were arrested for their part in it, but Cornell had escaped arrest and was still on the loose. A few nights later, Ron and I were in the Widow's pub which was owned by a woman named Madge. This public house was in Tapp Street, not far from the Beggars in Whitechapel Road. A few of our firm were present in the pub—Ian Barrie from Edinburgh, "Scotch" Jack Dickson from Glasgow, and other friends who were not exactly on the firm but drank with us regularly. These included the Teale brothers who were later to stand in the witness box against us, with the other Judases.

Ron, who at this time had not even had a drink, produced a piece of paper from his pocket and said to me, "This is a list of people that we should deal with. They have taken liberties long enough." I looked at the paper, and at the top of the list was the name George Cornell. I nodded in agreement, and then, without another thought, Ron said, "I'm going to see if that bastard Cornell is in the Beggars."

Ron then said to Ian Barrie, "Have you got a shooter on you, Ian?"

Ian said, "Yes."

Ron then said to him, "Come with me, Ian. We'll see if Cornell is in the Beggars." He added to Scotch Jack, "Drive us to the Beggars, Jack."

I said to Ron, "Let's talk about it first."

Ron replied, "There's nothing to talk about. I'm going to do the bastard."

They left the pub, and I ordered a gin and tonic. About ten minutes later, Ron, Ian and "Scotch" Jack returned. Ron said to me, "Get me a drink, I've just done the slag." It seemed ironic to me that Ron had gunned down Cornell in accordance with the sequence of the list he'd shown me earlier.

Ron told me what had happened. "Scotch" Jack had waited in the car outside the Beggars pub while Ron and Ian walked into the saloon bar. Cornell was sitting at the end of the bar with three associates. A record was playing, peculiarly enough entitled *The Sun Ain't Gonna Shine Any More*. Cornell, who had a drink in his hand, saw Ron approaching him from the door of the saloon bar, and just had time to say, "Look who's here," before Ron drew a Luger gun out of his right-hand overcoat pocket, levelled it at Cornell's head and fired.

Two of Cornell's associates dived to the floor, but Cornell's reactions were slower, and a 9 mm bullet hit him squarely in the centre of the forehead. Ian Barrie at the same time had pulled out an automatic and fired two bullets into the wall above the heads of where Cornell's associates had been standing. Cornell was dead before he even hit the floor, killed instantly by the bullet from the Luger.

Two or three other people in the parallel bar hit the deck a bit lively, out of fright and common sense, and the barmaid screamed loudly. Ron and Ian then turned about and left the way they came in, calmly got into the car and were driven back to Madge's pub by "Scotch" Jack.

The sequel to the story is that the record had jammed at the same time as the bullet hit Cornell in the forehead, and kept repeating, "The sun ain't gonna shine any more."

I decided there and then that we should all move away from Madge's pub and go to the Chequers public house in Walthamstow. We all got into different cars and made our way there, but before we left, I sent one of the firm to get a clean, complete set of clothes for Ron. They were to be brought to the Chequers so that he could change all of his clothing in case he got a pull by the law. Then the forensic experts would not be able to find any powder marks. I also told Ron to scrub his hands at the Chequers, and dispatched another member of the firm to drive over near the Beggars to see what he could find out.

This member of the firm did report back to me later on at the Chequers, and told me he had seen an ambulance take away a body on a stretcher to the nearby London Hospital. He also told me that road blocks and barriers were set up in the area of the Beggars, and that he had seen a Scotland Yard inspector going into the pub.

Ron's Luger was disposed of by Charlie Bateman, alias Charlie Clark, who we used to call the "Cat Man". We'd known him since the fifties and he proved to be a trustworthy friend right up to the end of his life. Only a couple of years ago, I read of his death in a Kent newspaper which a friend had sent to me. The article read, "Murder Remand: a Dover man appeared in court on Monday charged with murdering a disabled pensioner. Shane Keeler, eighteen, unemployed, is accused of murdering Charlie Bateman, seventy-one, who was found dead at his Dover home on Friday. Keeler was remanded in custody until next Wednesday.'

What the write-up didn't say was that during the fifties and early sixties, Charlie was one of the best cat burglars in London, and he used to drink and dine out with Ron and me and the rest of the firm every night. He was about six feet tall and looked like Gary Cooper in his younger days. I would bet the kid Shane Keeler didn't have a clue who Bateman really was. He used to loan out his bungalow in Chingford to Ron and me for meets and parties. He and his wife Sylvia kept at least a dozen cats there. Charlie was also a compulsive gambler. In his old age, he had moved away from London for a little peace, but the violence of the big city finally followed him out to the garden of England—Kent.

To return to the night of the Cornell shooting, we asked the tenant of the Chequers if we could use his private room upstairs so that we could have a few drinks and sandwiches. He agreed. We were good customers, and he was also a friend. So we made ourselves comfortable and settled back to discuss the demise of Cornell. We also put the nine o'clock news on the radio. It was announced that there had been a fatal shooting in an East End public house called the Blind Beggar. It was said that an expert marksman had shot dead a rival in gang warfare, and the police were making strenuous enquiries.

At this particular time, Ron and I were living in a flat in the Lea Bridge Road area, near Leyton. Some weeks after the shooting, Ron, I and others in the firm were having a late-night party in the flat when ladders appeared at the windows, and police came rushing in from all directions, in plain clothes and uniform. Some were armed with revolvers. They were led by a Chief Inspector Butler who said we were to go with him to Leyton police station where we would be placed on an identification parade for the murder of George Cornell.

I had already seen the barmaid of the Beggars and had quietly told her that it would be in her interest to forget what she had seen on the night of the shooting. I had also given her a few quid which I hoped would help to keep her happy.

We went to the station, and having had a few drinks, I sang a few songs in the cold cells with another couple of the firm before falling off to sleep. One of the songs was *Maybe It's Because I'm a Londoner*.

A few hours later, we were placed on the identification parade. The barmaid walked by and did not pick anyone out. Neither did the two brewery salesmen who had been present on the night of the shooting. So, much to the annoyance of Inspector Butler, he had to release us.

We went back to the flat where the press were waiting for us, asking for interviews. Ron and I told them of our innocence in no uncertain terms.

CHAPTER 5

FROM THE TOP OF THE WORLD . . . TO THE END OF THE LINE

The law, by this time, had got the right needle with us, so Ron and I decided we should go to Tangier to get out of the way for a while. Ian Barrie said he would like to come, too. We decided to hire a small plane off the coast at Dover, and we stayed the night in a hotel there.

The flight was organized so as to avoid the customs and the police at any of the London airports. We were ushered through customs by our pilot as arranged—part of his fee was for organizing this.

After a lot of journeying, we ended up in Tangier, Morocco, where we met our old friend and influence Billy Hill at his villa, just on the outskirts of the town. He and his wife Gypsy made us very welcome. We could not have wished for better hosts. A few days later, a friend of mine, Christine, joined us from London. She brought news that the police were going round the London haunts trying to get people to make statements against us. This gave us added incentive to stay in Tangier.

Christine had a good nature and a likeable personality, and I was pleased to have her as my constant companion. She is still one of my best friends today.

We would drink each night in Churchill's, the club Bill and Gypsy ran in the middle of Tangier. Churchill's was the best club in Tangier. Bill had bought the place to give to Gypsy as a special kind of toy. He told me this over a drink one night. The clientele was fascinating. Rich Arabs in white flowing gowns used to frequent the place, sitting at the tables deep in conversation while a band played music. One of the most popular tunes was *Strangers in the Night*.

The flower boys used to wait outside the club each night for Ron, Ian, Christine and myself to arrive. They would sell us bunches of the most beautiful blooms which we gave to Gypsy. Gypsy owned two large poodles which would keep her company in the club. They would not let anyone go near her. She wore the loveliest jewellery I have ever seen. Bill thought the world of her, and showered her with gifts. They were a charming couple. He was one of the best gamblers in the world. He made a fortune out of it, as well as being one of the most successful criminals ever to come out of London.

Bill arranged for us to have an apartment on the edge of Tangier. It was just a hundred yards from the beach. We would go swimming and sunbathing each day, and would sometimes drive to the centre of the town where we would use one of the best hotels and the adjoining open-air swimming pool. We would also visit the Casbah and frequent various different clubs in the area.

Billy had a white MG sports car at the time, as well as a saloon car. He would take us in the open-top to some of the remote parts of the 500-mile-long beach. Early each evening, we would sit and sip Turkish coffee outside the cafés before starting the night at Bob's Bar, a sleazy little club in the centre of Tangier. It was owned by Billy, but run by his frontman Bob, a little character from England.

We would drink at the small tables whilst Bill would roll a few joints of cannabis, and records played behind the bar. Young boy shoe-shiners would arrive at the club and suggest they attend to our shoes while we sat drinking. We were only too pleased to give them a few coins in payment. They were very intelligent, these Arab kids, very streetwise and likeable.

They showed a good sense of humour and could speak fluent English.

All in all, we were having a marvellous time. Ron still remembers this as his favourite country. It reminded him of Biblical times. He was particularly fascinated by the customary dress with the women in yashmaks, the donkeys, the dancing boys, the Casbah, and the atmosphere of Tangier itself.

But it was not to last. Ron, Ian, Christine and I were at the apartment one day when a knock came at the door. Christine answered it, and two plain-clothes Moroccan police told her they wished to speak to Mr Kray. I went to the door and they gave me a green form which said that Ron and I were to be interviewed at the local police station. These police were very polite. They were gentlemen. I told them we would soon be along to the police station, and they left.

Billy was friendly with a young Moroccan police detective, so we contacted Billy without delay and asked him to find out what was going on and why the police wanted to interview us. He said he would do his best.

Some time later, Billy came to the apartment and told us that Scotland Yard wanted us for the murder of Cornell, and had asked the Moroccan police to unofficially extradite us from Tangier. Bill said the best he could do was to get a stay of execution order for a period of forty-eight hours. His friend, the young detective, and a colleague would then take us to the airport and return us to London.

When our forty-eight hours were up, Ron, Ian, Christine and I had a drink with these two policemen at the airport. Bill's friend said he regretted that our stay in Tangier had to be halted, but he was obliged to follow orders from the top. He wished us luck, shook hands and escorted us on to the plane. We finally ended up back at London Airport, where there was no incident.

In the following weeks, we heard continuing rumours of police inquiries into our activities, but nothing too unusual happened and we were soon back in our old routines.

The year was 1966, and we were welcome at some of the

most famous and exclusive clubs and restaurants in London. There we mixed with many influential people including an MP who was being blackmailed. I won't mention his name, but he told Ron that he was being blackmailed by a boy who had in his possession various compromising letters. Ron didn't bully the boy; he asked him nicely, and he got the letters back. The MP was very grateful.

One of our favourite rendezvous was a restaurant/club called Quaglino's, just off Regent Street at the back of Jermyn Street. One night Ron was drinking and having a meal in there when he noticed Harold Wilson, the Prime Minister, sitting at a nearby table with his entourage of Special Branch men. I believe one of these men recognized Ron and, as it would not be good publicity for the Prime Minister to be seen in the same restaurant as my brother, Wilson and his group left hurriedly before ordering a meal. Ron also had dinner in the Houses of Lords and Commons with Lord Boothby and Manny Shinwell.

Another place we used to visit regularly was a very exclusive gambling club in Curzon Street, Mayfair. Then there was the Astor, the Connolly Club, L'Hirondelle and the Pigalle in Regent Street. We would wine and dine in all of these clubs until the early hours, but my favourite of all was the Society Restaurant Club in Jermyn Street. It had the most beautiful décor and silverware I have ever seen, and the nephew of the top politician Sir Alec Douglas-Home would play the piano in the foyer. It was a real classy place, and our American guests would love it when we took them there for the evening.

We once took the late Nat King Cole's wife to the Society. She was a very attractive person, and on this night was wearing some beautiful jewellery. One of our group wanted to follow her back to the hotel and steal it from her. I told him she was a guest of ours and to forget the idea.

Another night, we took to the Society one of the most fascinating characters I have met in my life. He was the late Barney Ross, the former lightweight champion of the world and a legend in his own lifetime.

His life story had been immortalized in a film, *Monkey On*

My Back. It told how, as a small child, he saw his father being robbed and shot dead. This experience made him a very aggressive young boy, and he would always be fighting with the other kids. He eventually channelled his aggression into boxing and became lightweight champion. He then went into the army and fought on the beaches of the South Pacific where he won an award for bravery, but was wounded. On the way back to the United States by boat, he was in so much pain from his wounds that he broke into the drugs area of the medical room, and stole cocaine. And so he became addicted to cocaine.

On arrival back in New York, he was given a hero's welcome and drove through the city in one of a cavalcade of cars, while he was showered with ticker-tape paper. But cocaine, and then the use of heroin, took their toll on him, his wife divorced him, and he fell so low in life that he became a hobo.

One scene in the film shows him walking down an alleyway with the snow falling, only to be attacked by a couple of muggers. This brings him alive again, he knocks both assailants out and leaves them sprawling amongst the old dustbins and garbage.

He then went to a medical centre where he took the cold-turkey cure and eventually beat the drugs. And years later, there he was sitting with us in the Society! As kids, we had read all the stories about this legend. He was short, thickset and had a broken nose and grey hair. He always wore dark glasses. On this night, he asked me if he could play the piano in the Society, so I got the announcer to introduce him over the mike. I don't know why, but I expected him to play jazz. Instead, he sat down and played the most beautiful classical music, and at the end, the whole room erupted into applause for this dignified little man.

We also met Maxie Rosenbloom, the ex-light heavyweight champion of the world, when he came to London from New York in 1966. We took him to all the clubs, such as the Pigalle. As well as being a great fighter, he had played many film roles in the fifties, usually acting the part of a convict. He had been a guest of US presidents and had also met the Pope. He told me many intriguing stories of his career and personal life. Sad to say, he died in an American lunatic asylum not even knowing who he was. He had no idea he had been a world champion when he was finally counted out for good.

Ron and I were always thrilled and proud to meet these heroes of our childhood, and never more so than when we went to Cardiff in 1966 and met the great boxing legend Jimmy Wilde.

Ron, Ian Barrie, Christine and myself were in Wales helping to organize a charity event for the Aberfan disaster fund at Cardiff Town Hall. The day after the show, a local Cardiff man called Bill Mayland took the four of us to a coal mine in the area, and we went down to pit face which was an interesting experience. We had gone down late in the afternoon, and by the time we got back up, darkness had fallen. When we did go out into the night to start our journey back to the city centre, the thing that struck me most was the beauty of the night stars which, after being down in the bowels of the earth, seemed more vivid than ever.

We had one more trip to make, just outside Cardiff, before our return to London. That journey led us to an old people's home where we made the pilgrimage to see Jimmy Wilde, the former flyweight champion of the world. Because of his frail build and hard punching power, he was known as "the ghost with a hammer". When Ron and I were kids, we used to regularly read a boxing instruction book which was written by Jimmy Wilde.

A male nurse let us into the ward and took us to see the great man himself. He had twinkling blue eyes and a warm handshake when we met him, and I noted that he had powerful hands for a little man. Christine sat holding his hand, and his blue eyes twinkled all the more. When it was time for us to leave, he did not seem keen to let go of Christine's hand, and she gave him a kiss on the cheek. He was the greatest fighter Wales ever produced.

Back in London, Ron and I used to spend a great deal of time in the company of boxing champions, including household names like Sonny Liston and Joe Jouis, and we had many friends within show-business circles too.

Ron and I actually did get involved with a pop group, briefly, in the sixties. They were called the Shots, and they released a single, *Keep A Hold Of What You've Got*, on Columbia, which unfortunately didn't set the world alight. We put them in the charge of a show-business man called Jack Segal, a Jewish friend of ours. They were just starting to do really well when Jack was killed in a car crash in the South of France. Ron and I then sold the group, and we later heard that they'd disbanded.

Throughout 1966, we kept up our fund-raising work, and confined ourselves to promoting variety or boxing shows because these were the areas we knew best. Some years earlier, we'd ventured out of our territory by promoting two wrestling shows in Bethnal Green and Canning Town, and those were memorable for reasons that the sport's officials would not appreciate!

At the time, two men called Martin and Dowell had the monopoly on wrestling, and they sent representatives of the board of officials to our show at the York Hall Public Baths, Bethnal Green. These reps told us there was not to be any kicking, butting or gouging, as they were against the rules. I believe that Martin and Dowell hoped that they would spoil our show by having strict enforcements imposed upon us. So I told the wrestlers to break all the rules on this particular night, as it was going to be the last show anyway.

They did. They really enjoyed themselves, gouging at eyes and kicking and butting each other to their hearts' content. As part of the show, I had arranged for a boxer, our friend Bobby Ramsey, to go into the ring with a wrestler called Chopper, which created a lot of interest. In that contest, Chopper got Ramsey in a leg hold in the first round, and I shouted out to Ramsey, "Bite him!" Ramsey did; he bit the wrestler in the leg and Chopper released his leg hold. Ramsey then knocked Chopper out in the second round with a left hook. I should point out that Ramsey had gloves on and Chopper had bare hands.

On the same night, we slung two wrestlers out of the ring for not trying. We reckoned they had been deliberately slipped in to spoil the show. I'm glad to say, that was my last attempt to be a wrestling promoter!

Our own clubs were continuing to bring in a few quid, although by 1966 we no longer had the Double R, the Kentucky or Esmerelda's Barn. The law did what they said they would after the Ronnie Marwood affair; they kept an eye on all our clubs, and I'm sure it wasn't coincidence that we started running into licensing problems after that. But we had plenty of other club interests, and we always managed to keep several steps ahead of the law.

We also managed to continue with a bit of travelling, despite having been extradited from Tangier. We'd already seen quite a lot of the world—Germany, Italy, Turkey, Ibiza, Casablanca, Guernsey, Jersey, Ireland, Switzerland, Spain, Holland, Greece and Gibraltar, as well as Enugu and Tangier. To this day, Ron's two outstanding memories of Istanbul, Turkey, are visits he made to two very different places: a brothel and a mosque! His favourite place was Morocco, but he was also very fond of Jersey. It's marvellous. It has lovely beaches and countryside, smashing hotels and nice restaurants.

Now, an American called Alan Cooper arranged for Ron to go to Paris and then America with Dickie Morgan. The purpose of the trip to America was to meet up with some of our Mafia contacts.

The Mafia had heard about the Kray twins quite some time before, and we had entertained various bosses in London. Earlier in 1966, we had met Angelo Bruno, the Philadelphia boss. He told me something I have always remembered and still often quote: "If you kick the dog, you kick the master." Those were his special words to anyone with the audacity to insult any member of his exclusive circle of friends. The unfortunate culprit would always get the message.

Ron also told me of a conversation that made an impact on him during his short trip to New York when he met Punchy Illiano, a Mafia don. The meeting took place at one of Illiano's night clubs. Punchy was a friend of Crazy Joe Gallo, the New York Mafia chief, and his brothers Larry and Al Gallo. Ron did not know for sure if there were any other brothers, so he said to Punchy, "How many brothers are in the family?" Punchy answered, "Joe, Larry, Al and me."

At that time, Ron and I were having discussions with the Mafia with a view to doing a bit of business, but we were arrested before anything came of it.

But the major event of 1966 for Ron and me was the springing of Frank "The Mad Axeman" Mitchell from Dartmoor. We decided to do this because the authorities would not give Frank a release date. He was serving years and years without any light at the end of the tunnel, without any indication of when he was coming out. I had already made one unusual visit to Dartmoor that year.

It had been reported in various newspapers that a prison warden working in Dartmoor had been sentenced for three months for taking bottles of Scotch and tobacco into the jail for the cons and that the address and phone number of Ronald Kray, a London gangster, had been found in the warder's possession. At this time, Ron and I had some friends, including Frank, serving time in Dartmoor. It was made known to us that we were barred from visiting the prison, on the assumption that we had bribed the warder to take in the Scotch and tobacco. I had promised my friends in Dartmoor that I would organize some sort of entertainment. I intended to keep this promise, though I realized I would have to visit Dartmoor by guile and by using an alias.

I contacted Ted "Kid" Lewis, the former welterweight champion of the world, a legend in boxing, and asked him if he would accompany me to Dartmoor to give a talk to the prisoners there about his career. I also arranged to show films of all his old fights, borrowed from a film distribution company in Wardour Street.

At my request, Kid Lewis sent the prison governor a letter stating that he would like to visit Dartmoor to show his films. He also stated that he would be accompanied by three friends who would be helping him to show the films. Some time later, he received a letter of approval.

I saw the funny side of this, and decided to take along two fellers from the East End who had a long list of convictions for various offences. This was my way of challenging the ban on my entry into Dartmoor.

That day, we reached the prison by car. I was pleased that it was pouring really hard with rain, and we were pushed through the prison courtyard without being checked out properly. We eventually reached the area where the films were to be shown, and Kid Lewis received a standing ovation from the cons. At the end of his talk and the films, he wept with emotion. He was, at this time, in his seventies.

After the show, the governor, the padre and their entourage escorted us to a large hut and gave us a splendid meal. They seemed to really enjoy telling me about the various convicts. At the end of the meal, they shook us warmly by the hands and said, "Don't forget to call again." I said we would give this some consideration.

I did find out at a later date that our ruse became known to the authorities. It was the first and only time that I had ever been barred from a prison. On reflection, I wish this ban had been enforced for a longer period of time!

I didn't return to Dartmoor myself for the freeing of the "Axeman" on 12 December. We sent Big Albert Donaghue and Joe Williams. They went in a car and were to wait for Frank at a pre-arranged point at Bagga Tor. The idea was that Frank would escape, write letters to the newspapers protesting at not being given a release date, and would then give himself up.

It was not difficult for Frank to make his escape, because he regularly went on outdoor working parties on the moor. He would ride the wild ponies like a cowboy, and hitch his pony to the door of a nearby inn while he went in to have a pint or two of his favourite mild and bitter and a Cornish pasty. The works party screw would keep watch for Frank during his stay at the inn to make sure that all was clear and that these drinking sprees would not be tumbled. I personally feel this all added to the drama of the occasion for Frank. It was hardly necessary, because all the villagers were aware of the gentle giant's drinking habits at the inn. But it was all part of Frank's humour to assign a screw to a job of work.

Frank was back in London before he was even missed at Dartmoor. We kept him out of the way, at the flat of a friend of ours, Lennie Dunn. He wasn't short of company. "Scotch" Jack Dickson was with him a lot of the time as well as "Mad" Teddy Smith and Billy Exley, an ex-boxer. We also provided Frank with a blonde girlfriend.

Teddy Smith wrote Frank's letter to the Home Secretary. We posted copies to the *Daily Mirror* and *The Times* and waited for a response. There was none. All we wanted was a promise that Frank's case would at least be investigated. But no statement of any kind was forthcoming from the Home Office, so this meant that Frank had to stay on the run. . . .

It has been said by some writers and ghostwriters that Frank is still alive. I am sad to say this is ridiculous. It was blatantly obvious during the trial—when I was acquitted of his murder—that certain people were trying to get me blamed for Mitchell's death. Billy Exley gave false evidence against me to this end. Yet he and three Greeks were responsible for murdering Frank.

They had been trying to get him out of the country with a false passport on 23 December. But for various reasons, an argument started between Exley and Mitchell. Exley and the Greeks pulled out guns and shot Mitchell several times.

This part of the story filtered through to me some time later. I heard that Frank Mitchell was so strong he was still alive after being shot three or four times—until Exley fired a bullet into his head. Mitchell never did like Exley.

The sad story of Frank Mitchell reminds me of the novel *Of Mice and Men*. He had got so close to his freedom. And whenever I hear the song *The Green, Green Grass of Home* by Tom Jones it makes me very sad, as that too reminds me of Frank. Sometimes life can be very sorrowful, and the story of the "Mad Axeman" is one of those occasions.

With Frank Mitchell, Christmas and the New Year behind

us, we became involved in yet another confrontation with the law—although in this one, the tables were turned. In April 1967, a CID man, Detective Sergeant Leonard Townsend, appeared in the Old Bailey. He was charged with demanding £50 a week from Ron in return for him seeing that the police would leave us alone in a certain public house we used. As a matter of principle, Ron refused to give evidence in court, even against a copper, and so he had to go into hiding for a while.

They issued a warrant for his arrest, to force him into the witness stand in court, but he wasn't found, and he never did give the evidence they wanted.

In the summer of that year, there seemed to be some hope of Frances and me getting back together. She had been in hospital following her breakdown and had come out to her sister-in-law's flat in Shoreditch. I went to see her there on 6 June. We were getting ready to go on holiday to Ibiza the following morning. Our cases were packed and we were all ready to go.

On this particular night, Frances had been to the hairdresser's earlier on, but she couldn't get her hair straight and this was bothering her. I could see she was terribly upset, so I phoned a friend of ours, Adele, who was a woman hairdresser. I asked her if she could get round to see Frances that night, but she said she wouldn't be able to make it.

I said goodbye to Frances and said I would see her in the morning. As I drove off back to Watney Street, where I was staying at the time, I had an uneasy feeling about Frances, and I was going to drive back and see her again. But as I got to Bethnal Green Road, I saw Sammy Lederman walking along the pavement, so I stopped the car and gave him a lift. He also lived near Watney Street. This seemed to take away my uneasy feeling for a bit, and I ended up going to sleep at about 10 pm.

The following day, I went back to the flat in Shoreditch and rang the doorbell but could get no answer. I saw the window open and I was going to climb through, but I hesitated. I did not want any conflict with my in-laws.

I then drove off to Kingsland Road where I normally had my hair cut, and while I was waiting in the chair for my turn, I had a strange premonition of a funeral in procession. Somehow I knew it was the funeral of Frances. I could see it all there before me.

When I left the barber's, I went back to the flat in Shoreditch and one of the friends of Frankie Shea, my brother-in-law, came towards me as I pulled up in the car. He told me in faltering words that something had happened and that Frances was dead.

I went into the flat and the police were there. I was told that Frances had committed suicide by taking an overdose of barbiturate tablets. There was no last note anywhere in sight, which I found hard to believe because on the last two attempts, she had left notes. I was suspicious of my father-in-law, who had been first on the scene. I thought he might have picked up a letter or note.

I found it very difficult to believe that Frances was no longer with me. That weekend, I went back down to the caravan site near Southend where we had spent so many nice weekends, and I visited the small antique shops where we used to go and have a look around, so that I could try to imagine that she was still with me. I was so sad that in one of the shops I became overcome with grief, to the great concern of the shopkeeper. I saw all the little boats with sails on the quayside at the village of Stowe. All this brought back memories.

The worst part of all was not so much the funeral but a week later when I collected all Frances's personal possessions and clothing from her mother's flat, and took them back to Watney Street to sort out. I could still smell the sweet body scent of Frances on some of her clothes.

It was a terrible time. And the events which followed in that year only led to more terrible times ahead. By now, Ron and I were only a matter of months away from the arrests which would send us to prison for a recommended minimum of thirty years, in my case for the murder of Jack "The Hat" McVitie.

When McVitie and I were released from Wandsworth, back at the beginning of the sixties, we often met in North and East London, and he would do odd jobs for Ron and me from time to time. But he was not very reliable because he was prone to heavy bouts of drinking which made him volatile. On more than one occasion, I had to warn him for upsetting friends of mine, including Freddie Foreman and Ronnie Olives from South London. McVitie once went into one of Foreman's clubs in the Balham area and caused a scene. Fred was very upset at this, so I had to warn McVitie that he was messing with the wrong people who, moreover, were friends of ours.

Another time, he caused trouble in the Log Cabin Club in Wardour Street, Soho, which was owned by the East London heavyweight fighter Billy Walker and his brother George. During the scuffle that followed, McVitie was lucky to come away with cut hands when he clashed with Ron Olives.

The last straw—and McVitie's undoing—was the night he went into the Regency Club and threatened the owner of the club, John Barry, and his brother. McVitie was drunk and brandishing a sawn-off shotgun, issuing threats, including threats to Ron and me. McVitie knew that Ron and I were silent partners in the club so, to me, he had taken one liberty too many.

The Barry brothers were terrified. They complained to me of McVitie's drunken and threatening behaviour. So a couple of nights later, I made a point of going to the Regency Club, figuring I would see McVitie there. I was right. McVitie was at the bar. I sidled up to him, bought him a drink, and proceeded to sound him out. On this particular night, he was reasonably sober so I thought I would find out how bold he would get.

I said, "I missed you the other night when you came in with a shotgun."

He replied, "Yes, I was surprised you wasn't here, too."

I said, "You know we are in this club, so you shouldn't cause any trouble in here."

He replied, without an apology, "Those two bastards (the Barry brothers) tried to block me coming in here. They said I had had too much to drink."

I said, "The other night when you were waving your shotgun about, you also asked where I was."

"That's right, I wondered where you was," he replied.

I had repeatedly warned McVitie, and I knew it was only a matter of time before he had to go. I said: "I want to talk to you in the restaurant upstairs."

McVitie joined me in a Chinese meal upstairs. I ordered chicken chow mein and curry. During the meal, I quietly discussed with McVitie the number of people he had upset in the past few months. He was very arrogant. I paid for the meal, knowing it was to be his last. This may seem quite callous, but one must take into account that McVitie was over the age of twenty-one, so he knew what he was doing.

I knew that if I just hurt McVitie by cutting him with a knife, he would use a shotgun to gain his revenge, if I allowed him the chance. He had, in the past, taken shots at a feller called Tommy Flanagan during a row in the Regency. Another time he had cut someone in the basement of the Regency with a knife and had then walked upstairs to the upper bar and wiped the bloody knife all over the dresses of women who were drinking at the bar.

In short, one learns in the East End environment the rules for survival, and I knew that it was a matter of survival of the most ruthless. I was going to be the most ruthless, because my survival instinct was strong, due to the fact that I had plenty of practice growing up in the East End amongst some hard and cunning company.

During my conversation with McVitie at the restaurant, he continued to talk himself into an early grave. He said: "When you had the row with the Watney Street firm years ago, I made one with them, and I was sitting with Jimmy Fullerton and the others waiting for you while we had a drink in the Crown pub in Chrisp Street, Poplar. We were all tooled up, and a few of us had shooters. It was Bulla Ward who marked our card that you, Ron and the firm were going to cut Jackie Martin that night."

I replied, "It's a pity we missed you and the others, but we did cop for Martin's brother, Terry. As you know, the bastard signed statements and got Ron, Ramsey and Billy Jones plenty of bird, so you were on a bad firm. But you never learn, do you? Hope you enjoyed the meal. I'll see you around." I then left the Regency that October night knowing that the next time I saw "The Hat" I would kill him.

They called McVitie "The Hat", because he was bald on the crown of his head, with thick hair at the sides, so he always wore a hat. He was a pretty good dresser. He was about five feet nine and a half, big-boned with large hands. He wouldn't hesitate to use a tool or a shooter. He once broke a woman's back, and was adept at armed robbery.

The following day, I marked Ron's card that I had seen "The Hat" and had a drink with him. I also told Ron of the conversation, and about my intentions that "The Hat" should go. Ron agreed.

That same night, Ron and I and some of the firm drove in cars to 167 Evering Road, Stoke Newington, an address where a woman friend by the name of Carol rented the basement. A group of us went inside and settled down for a drink. We had earlier been in a pub close to Vallance Road where we had stocked up with more alcohol. I had a Biretta automatic in my pocket. I told Ron I was going to the Regency, which was nearby, to see if I could find "The Hat", and if so, I was going to shoot him. I got in a Cortina, one of the many cars we used. I entered the Regency and glanced around the main bar, which was upstairs, but could not see "The Hat". So I went to the office. Johnny Barry and his brother were sitting behind the desk.

I said to them, "Is 'The Hat' in the basement? See if he's down there and tell the cunt I want to see him now."

Both the Barrys went white. My intention was to shoot "The Hat" as soon as he entered the office. The noise of the band playing downstairs on the floor below would have drowned out any sound from the .22. I was not concerned about the Barrys being witnesses to the shooting. I believe they sussed me out.

Parky went down to the basement to see if "The Hat" was there. Just before he left, I warned him, "Don't mark his card that I'm in a bad mood. Just be relaxed when you talk to him." I said to John Barry, who was still sitting behind the desk, "Just leave things to me and everything will be OK. Make sure no one walks in here once 'The Hat' gets here."

As I said, John Barry was white and nervous, and I guess he had a fair idea what I had on my mind. He just nodded his head in assent and said no more. After about five minutes, Parky returned and said he had found out that "The Hat" had been in earlier but had since left.

I told Parky and his brother John that I would be leaving, but if "The Hat" came back to the club, they should be nice to him and buy him a few drinks. They should not crack on to him that I had been looking for him, but should phone me at Carol's in Evering Road where I would be having a drink. John and Parky seemed relieved and just nodded in agreement. I then left the club and went back to Carol's where I told Ron the score. Ron and I had a little argument; Ron said I was a mug to go looking for him in the Regency.

Tony Lambrianou, another friend and member of the firm, was also in the basement having a drink, so I said to him, "I want you to go to the Regency and see if you can see 'The Hat'. If you do, then get him to come back here. Tell him there's a good party going on, but don't tell him Ron and I are here. Try to make sure he doesn't bring anybody else with him. Just pal up with him and buy him a few drinks to keep him happy.'

Lambrianou left and I then told Ronnie Hart, a cousin of ours who had also joined the firm and would later give evidence against us, to go upstairs and keep watch from the street door. I asked him to let me know when Lambrianou returned, and whether or not "The Hat" was with him. I intended to shoot him as soon as he walked into the basement. I had told Ron and the others what I was going to do, and that they should not interfere. They should just leave it to me.

The other people in the room were Ron, Ronnie Bender, Ronnie Hart, and two other fellers who will remain nameless. The group of us were drinking, while soul records were playing, quietly. About twenty minutes later, Hart came back down from where he'd been keeping watch. He said he'd just seen "The Hat" with Lambrianou whose brother Chris was with them. Also in the company were two friends of "The Hat", the Mills brothers Ray and Alan. They were two thieves and up-and-coming villains, but I knew we could handle them and "The Hat". As they entered the room, McVitie seemed surprised to see Ron and me. He said, "I heard there was a party here, and Chris invited me along."

I said, "Sit down, I want to talk to you." I also said to the Mills brothers, "Don't interfere and you will be OK."

I said to McVitie, "I warned you more than once about causing trouble for us, but you didn't listen. I told you about the trouble you had in Fred's club."

McVitie replied, "Fred's club was nothing to do with you."

I then pulled out the automatic, placed it to his head and pulled the trigger. There was a click of the hammer against the firing pin, but the gun jammed. McVitie dived towards the window at the back of the room in an attempt to escape, whilst the two Mills brothers froze and stood where they were. Ron and Hart pulled McVitie back into the centre of the room, and I said to them, "Leave him to me." McVitie made a grab for his pocket where I knew he had a knife, so I grabbed hold of him and butted him in the face.

I had, in the meantime, put the useless automatic back in my pocket. As McVitie and I were struggling, we fell against a small table which had a plate on it full of cut-up pieces of lemon for the drinks. Beside it was a long kitchen knife which was there for slicing the lemon. I made a grab for the knife with my right hand, picked it up, switched it to my left hand, and brought it up into the right hand side of McVitie's body near the ribs. I heard a hiss-like breath being taken away from his body. I then plunged the knife like I was using a left hook to the head. The knife caught McVitie near the eye and he fell to the floor. I then plunged the knife into his body and I knew he was dead.

Ron Bender came over to McVitie's body, listened for his heart and said, "McVitie's dead."

There was a lot of blood on the floor. I told Hart to go upstairs and get a bed cover off one of the beds. We then cleaned the blood up, but before doing so, I told the Mills brothers to keep their mouths shut and to see me in Teddy Barry's pub at the end of the week, Friday.

Tony Lambrianou later said he had tried to get McVitie to the house on his own, but McVitie insisted that the Mills brothers and Chris Lambrianou went to the party with him. I should point out that Chris Lambrianou was eventually sentenced to life imprisonment along with Ron, Tony Lambrianou and myself, yet he never had a clue what was going to happen that night and never raised one finger against McVitie. He never even helped to clean the flat up. He was quite distressed and in a state of shock. Tony had not been able to mark his brother's card that a murder was going to take place.

Ron Bender and Hart wrapped up the body of McVitie and placed it in one of our several cars outside the house. I gave orders for the car to be driven to a certain place so that the body could be disposed of. We then split up, and Ron and I went to Harry Hopwood's flat in Hackney Road. I had a bath and made sure the knife I had used, and the automatic, were dumped in the canal nearby.

Ron and I then went to another friend's flat in North London until the following day when I drove us by car to a mansion in the country, which was owned by a close friend of ours. We stayed there a week, and then returned to London.

I would like to explain that the two nameless people who were present in the basement were two young friends of Ron's. They had accidentally wandered into the basement that night to see Ron and were innocent bystanders to the murder. The police did find out they were present, because the Judas Ronnie Hart made a statement to the police implicating them. But they stood up to the police interrogation like real men and refused to write a statement of any kind, even though they were issued with all kinds of threats and dire consequences. I heard, about ten years into my sentence, that one of these young fellers died from an overdose of drugs. This was not related to the murder in any way. I have lasting memories of them both, and they will forever remain in my heart as the good friends they were.

People still ask me today if I feel any remorse for the crime I committed. I have complex thoughts on this matter, not so much on the actual subject of remorse, but about why the establishment expects criminals to feel remorse for murder while at the same time expecting the soldier at war to feel victorious. Let's put it this way: if I had not killed Jack McVitie, he might be writing this instead of me, and I might be where he is.

In comparison, soldiers fighting in the Falklands, say, could justifiably pick out an Argentinian soldier on the skyline and squeeze the trigger. That would be the end of the Argentinian, who would most probably be a loving family man and not a villain like McVitie. The difference between the two individuals is like chalk and cheese, saint and sinner. And still, no one would ask the British soldier in the act of war if he felt any remorse for killing. If it was a matter of choice, I would sooner see the loss of the McVities of this world than the deaths of innocent young soldiers, plucked from the joys of life by the bullets of war.

As human beings, we have all got our failings, and one day we will all be judged. I feel sure that I won't be lonely on my journey, wherever it may lead.

Ron was recently asked by a researcher what his feelings were about our violent acts towards other villains in the fifties and sixties. His reply was this, "I never felt sorry for anyone who got hurt. They deserved it, otherwise it wouldn't have happened. We didn't enjoy violence, we tried to avoid it, but we had to use it sometimes.

"One feller called me a fat slob, so I had to do him. I went in the toilet and told someone I wanted to speak to him. As he came in, I cut him with a knife. He had to have plastic surgery.

"Another time, a straight man came to see me, and he told me that a feller from Mile End had broken his daughter's nose in three places because she wouldn't have sex with him. She was only fifteen. The Mile End feller also broke a seventeen-year-old boy's jaw in three places. So I phoned this feller up and told him I wanted to see him up Esmerelda's Barn. He was a dirty little rat. So I thought I'd set an example with him . . .

"We've both been violent in our time, me and Reggie, but we never liked it. It's like soldiers in the war, SAS and that. They're not violent people, really, but they have to use it. Our Uncle Albert told me he shot a few people when he was in the army, yet he was the most placid man I've ever met. He wouldn't have hurt a fly."

The police were busy during the rest of 1967 and the beginning of the next year. Various members of our firm were busy, too, giving statements against us to the law, telling lies about the McVitie and Cornell murders and the Frank Mitchell affair and making deals whereby they would obtain reduced sentences in return for the information they gave about Ron and me.

On 8 May 1968, Ron and I and a number of the firm went to Terry Barry's pub for a drink. It was one of the best nights I ever had, and at closing time we all got in several cars and went to the Astor Club off Berkeley Square. We continued drinking there until the early hours.

I noticed while we were there that flashlight bulbs seemed to be exploding all over the place. We were used to having our photographs taken when we went out, but so many was unusual and I mentioned this to Ron. I also noticed plain-clothes police detectives mingling in the club, but we were used to this, too, so we did not take much notice.

In the early hours, Ron and I drove back to Braithwaite House at Old Street, where we were living at the time. I went to bed with a young lady, and Ron was in the company of a young feller.

I was sleeping soundly and contentedly when something woke me up. I looked up from beneath the sheets to find the bed was surrounded by plain-clothes police, some holding revolvers and another with an iron bar. Chief Inspector "Nipper" Read was the leader of this howling mob. He said, "You are under arrest. Get out of bed with your hands in the air."

I thought this was rather embarrassing, because I was naked and lying next to a young lady. But I complied with his wishes, even though I could see how humorous I must have looked. Read proceeded to read out the many charges, which included murder. I was allowed to put on my trousers, shirt and shoes, and was then handcuffed and escorted to waiting cars in the street. I was driven to police headquarters where I was placed in a cell. Ron had been put through the same procedure and charged, too. It was the end of our reign.

CHAPTER 6

INSIDE STORIES

On 16 May 1969, after being sentenced, I was taken to the special unit in Brixton Prison to await my transfer to Parkhurst on the Isle of Wight. On the morning of the transfer, I was handcuffed and escorted to a waiting car in the prison yard.

Just as I was getting into the car, one of the detectives wanted to put a blanket over my head. He said this was to protect me from the photographers and the pressmen. Right away I objected and said to the copper, "I'm not having no fucking blanket over my head. I've nothing to be ashamed of. I'm not a fucking rapist, so take the fucking thing away from me." And I sat bolt upright in the back of the car in view of all.

The car was only one of a convoy which was to take me on my journey to Parkhurst. We sped along the roads, sirens going all the time. I am sure the driver of the car I was in was trying to worry me with the speed he was doing. As we travelled along, I thought of my late wife who died at the early age of twenty-three. And here I was at thirty-five, so I didn't care a fuck if the car crashed or not. So far, I had had a good life, and I was not going to let my sentence get me down.

I also noticed along the way that in the police car behind me, a plain-clothes detective was using a cine camera to film me on my journey. Though I resented this intrusion, I made no comment and we carried on towards the ferry that would take me to my new home on the Isle of Wight.

Ron had gone to Durham Prison, along with Ron Bender, Chris and Tony Lambrianou, and "Scotch" Ian Barrie. Charlie, our brother, was taken to Chelmsford and Freddie Foreman went to Leicester.

I arrived at the massive gates of Parkhurst, and the driver of the car I was in drove up the long path to the block that was to become my home for the best part of the next seventeen years.

We got out of the car, went through a little corridor that was partitioned off with bullet-proof glass, and ended up in a small office with a table, three chairs and a filing cabinet. A senior screw, who was with two others, signed a form to accept me from the Brixton screw I was handcuffed to, and I heard one of the screws say in a quiet voice to the other, "Did Richardson get his visiting form?" The other one answered, "Yes, he did." I knew that this was meant for my ears, as I knew that Eddie Richardson was at Parkhurst. Eddie and his brother Charlie were the leaders of the Richardson firm from south of the river. The screws had wanted to watch my reaction to the name Richardson, because they believed we were still enemies over the death of George Cornell, who was on their firm, and because of all the newspaper talk. But I was prepared for this sort of thing: I had learned that it was best not to react to psychology, so my features remained impassive.

I was then shown to the other side of the office door and into the prison wing where I was to start my sentence. One of the first people I noticed standing around the hotplate was Dennis Stafford, whose real name I knew to be Dennis Seigenberg. As I mentioned earlier, I had first met him in a gang fight when Ron and I were sixteen years of age. We had injured Stafford and two others, Roy Harvey and Walter Birch, in this fight in Hackney and had been charged with grievous bodily harm. We went to the Old Bailey and were acquitted. I found it ironic that all these years later, I would be in the same prison as Seigenberg and that he, too, would be serving a life sentence, in his case for shooting dead a fruit-machine operator in Newcastle.

Seigenberg nodded his head at me and I nodded back. I also spotted Tommy Wisby, one of the Great Train Robbers. I did not recognize him at first. He looked much older than the last time I met him in my club, the Kentucky, in 1963. Wisby said, "Hello, Reg. We guessed you or Ron would arrive here sooner or later."

I said, "Hello, Tom. Glad to see you, but I wish it wasn't in prison. It's a while since the Kentucky."

Wally "Angel Face" Probyn was also standing there. He introduced himself. I had not met him before, but I knew of his reputation and I recognized his face from photographs. He came from Hoxton, and he was serving fifteen years for a shotgun shooting. Years later, his part in the film *McVicar* was played by the actor and singer Adam Faith. It was Probyn who engineered the armed robber John McVicar's famous escape from prison and not McVicar.

I do not like McVicar. I first met him when I was in Brixton Prison, on remand with Ron, although I knew his name before that because he used to knock about with my brother-in-law. When we were walking round in circles for the daily exercise in Brixton, one could judge the slags from the genuine people and the nobodies from the somebodies by the clothing they wore. As I watched one day from the inner cirlce of the exercise yard, someone pointed out a couple of faces from the Hoxton manor, and with them was a feller in his early twenties who was dressed like a right slag. He looked like a garage hand.

Someone said it was John McVicar. Those who know McVicar will tell you that he was a mug as a criminal. In fact, he almost says the same in his own book.

When I was out in the fifties and sixties, I never saw him in any of the exclusive clubs of the time. He wouldn't have been allowed in.

When he writes about his so-called robbing days, he says he rode shotgun, as though he was Jesse James. Yet, my friend Billy Gentry who got nicked with him on a robbery told me that McVicar was sitting in the back of an old car with a worn-out shotgun. So his robbing days were far from glamorous.

I know it to be true that McVicar grovelled for parole. He says in his book that he forsook his own family by making up lies that his father was an alcoholic so as to get more chance of parole.

My friend Joe Martin, who is a lifer and was caught on the wall during McVicar's escape, gives all credit to Probyn who was the real hero.

In the past few years, McVicar has earned money by running down Ron amd me in articles. He once wrote that we put the torch to Frank Mitchell, yet we were acquitted of Frank Mitchell's murder. To try to blame us for this murder goes against basic criminal code, which he was supposed to live by at one time. He knows that he has not done our chances of parole any good, but I expect no more of him. He was never a true villain.

Last but not least, when he attended my mother's funeral in the role of reporter, he did not wear a tie. Afterwards, he wrote that he did not want to be recogised as one of the mourners. He also made derogatory remarks about what should be placed on Ron's tombstone.

I liked Probyn right away when I met him that first day in Parkhurst. He was anti-establishment, but very sociable, and he invited me to his cell later on for a cup of tea. I agreed to join him.

I also noticed a six-footer standing nearby, who looked a bit weird and out of place. He seemed to eye me very suspiciously. I checked on him later on, and found out that his name was Michael Copeland. He came from up north somewhere, and was in for stabbing to death three people. He was an ex-army man who was a keep-fit fanatic. I did not particularly like the look of him.

They say that first impressions are always the best, and this was to prove true, even though he half nodded his head towards me. I could see that he didn't like me, though, and some time later I was to have a fight with him.

Harry Roberts, who had killed three coppers by shooting them in Shepherds Bush, London, was also there to greet me.

He looked like his photos, and was very quiet and friendly. He, too, made me very welcome and said he would have a cup of tea with me some time.

The next person I saw was Billy Smith, who came walking down the iron staircase to where I was standing. I knew him from London. He was doing sixteen years for a robbery and like Probyn, he came from Hoxton. A couple of years earlier I had shot him in the leg in a club when we had a dispute, but he, too, greeted me cordially. In fact, I owed Smith a favour because during our trials at the Old Bailey, he got a message to us that the law wanted him to give evidence against us over the shooting and had offered him parole to do so, but he had politely told them to fuck off. I admired him for this and, as I write all these years later, I am still friends with Billy. He is now back on the street, I'm pleased to say.

Harry Roberts offered to show me the small prison garden, so I followed him out of the wing into an area with mounds of soil and a small glasshouse where tomatoes were growing. I saw a grey-haired, elderly feller sitting in a chair in just a pair of shorts, basking in the sunshine, and I was curious to know who he was, as he looked a little like Billy Daniels, the singer. Harry told me, "That's Peter Kroger who is doing forty years for selling atomic bomb plans to the Russians." Harry introduced me to him.

Nearby, Eddie Richardson was laying on the grass, sunbathing, and I stopped and gave him a few words of thanks. He and his brother Charlie had sent messages to the Old Bailey, offering us their help during our trial.

Throughout the day, I met the rest of the small group who were in this special security wing and with whom I would remain together a number of years. They were Roy James, another of the Great Train Robbers, and Billy Collins, an ex-lightweight fighter from the Hackney area of London, who was doing sixteen years. I knew of Collins. He had been done for a robbery, and though I had never met him previously, Ron and I had given his wife the defence money for his trial. Yet his wife ended up giving evidence against us in the McVitie trial.

Another feller called Cyril, a thief from Blackpool doing ten years, was the last of the bunch I was to meet that day.

One of the screws said, "Don't you get worried meeting all your old enemies?" At this, I made no comment. I was too preoccupied with getting to know my new surroundings to let any happenings of the past worry me, and I was definitely not going to let the screws wind me up. That night, I went into the small gym and watched some of the fellers working out with the weights. I had never been interested in weights in the past, but I decided to take up weightlifting and weight-training. More than twenty years later, I am still weight-training, though I leave out the heavy ones these days.

I'm proud to say that during my years at Parkhurst, I won three medals and thirty-two certificates at weightlifting. For one of these medals, which was presented with a shield, I represented Parkhurst in the Southern Area championships, with two other cons. One was a feller from Nottingham and the other was Roy Shaw. I'm told there is soon to be a film based on the life stories of Roy Shaw and Lenny Maclean, both friends of Ron and me and both professional street fighters from the East End of London. I am glad to say Roy Shaw has come a long way since his weightlifting days at Parkhurst.

I accepted my sentence from the day I started it, and so did Ron. The trial had lasted almost thirteen weeks, and it finished more than a year after our arrests. We each received a thirty-year sentence for the murders of Cornell on 9 March 1966, and McVitie on 29 October 1967. We were cleared of murdering Frank Mitchell, although I was found guilty of plotting his escape. Charlie, our brother, got ten years after being found guilty of getting rid of McVitie's body along with Freddie Foreman who wasn't even on the firm but was a close friend of Charlie.

Others who were also charged with various offences in the trials included Connie Whitehead, Big Albert Donaghue, Wally Garelick, Tommy Cowley, "Scotch" Jack Dickson, Pat Connolly, Ian Barrie, the Lambrianou brothers, Tony Barry and Ron Bender. Aside from the murder hearings, certain of these people were involved in other charges: conspiracy, planning and effecting the "Axeman" escape, being accessories to criminal offences and harbouring those involved in them.

Many of our former friends gave evidence against us, people like the ex-boxer Billy Exley, our own cousin Ronnie Hart and the slag Dickson. In the East End, we call these sort of people "weddings men". They like the weddings, but they want no part of the funerals in life. Some people had at least fifteen years of weddings with Ron and me, but when it came to the funeral, they fell by the wayside. Another Cockney word for their type is "screamers". They're OK when all is well, but they scream their heads off when things go badly.

When I saw the array of traitors against us at the Old Bailey, it did not affect me too much emotionally. Ron and I both took it in our stride, in that human nature is unpredictable. We also both accepted that we were the captains of the ship, so even though some of the crew had turned traitor, which was similar to mutiny, we would just have to take the responsibility for, and consequences of, choosing the wrong crew. We accepted their lying as a fact of life.

When we heard the sentence, with a recommendation of thirty years minimum, Ron and I were, again, not too emotional. We had been told while on remand at Brixton Prison that we were going to get this recommendation so the sentence came as no great surprise. We went back down to the cells below, Ron and I, and started to shadow box to get rid of some of our pent-up tension and frustration, Ron in one corner of the cell and me in the other.

I bear no malice or grudge against any of the police who arrested me or the judge who sentenced me. It was all part of their job. I do feel, though, that our sentences were too severe.

The first year in the special security block at Parkhurst passed quickly enough. I was then shifted to a security block at Leicester Prison, where I spent another year. And it was there that I first met Harry Johnson. He was the first person I saw on my arrival. Harry was short but reasonably thickset with balding fair hair, deep blue eyes and a little bulldog pug nose. He was known throughout all the prison world as "Hate 'Em All" Harry because he hated screws and cons alike. He had been in prison since 1964, and was sick of the company. Yet I found Harry to have exceptionally good principles and a marvellous sense of humour. He was also spotlessly clean in everyday appearance. We used to work out on the weights together.

It was also while I was in Leicester that I received a letter from Stubby Kaye. It reminded me of one particular night at the Stork Club in Swallow Street when I was joined by Stubby Kaye and Judy Garland. Stubby ad-libbed one of his famous song and dance routines while Judy and I enjoyed his act. That night I gave him a pair of cuff links. It was nice to hear from him in the less than carefree surroundings of Leicester Prison.

"Hate 'Em All" Harry and I were shifted back to the security block at Parkhurst where we remained together for some time. By this time Ron was waiting for me there. I would spend eight years with Ron at the Isle of Wight, five in the security block and three in the psychiatric wing. Ron then went to Broadmoor Hospital, where he still is today, and I spent five years in the Parkhurst hospital block.

In the early days, when Ron had come to the Isle of Wight, we used to pass our time with "Hate 'Em All" Harry and another good friend, Joe Martin. One day in the yard, a cop killer called Bill Skingle slung a sly punch at Harry over some difference of opinion, and they had a scuffle. Ron grabbed hold of Skingle, who had caught Harry off balance, and we broke it up. Harry said to Ron and me, "I will do that skinny bastard for that, but I'll let the slag think it's all over with first."

About three days later, Skingle was washing at one of the sinks when Harry hit him on the cheekbone with a small disc he had stolen out of the weight room, and gave him a broken cheekbone. At the time, I was in my cell. Harry calmly walked in and said, "Will you get shot of this piece of iron I've just done Skingle with, in case I get a pull for it?"

Skingle was taken to the hospital where he had an operation, and after that he kept ten feet away from "Hate 'Em All" at all times. Skingle is still serving natural life for shooting one copper nine times.

Joe Martin was serving life for murder committed during a robbery. We had been friends with him on the street so we were pleased that he came down from Durham Prison to Parkhurst. When he was in his early twenties, he was an exceptionally good amateur fighter.

One day, he and Ron were on the wing and it was time for Ron's medication. This particular day, the screw told Ron he would have to wait for his dose, and Ron saw this as unreasonable. He needed the medication to keep him calm so he had an argument with the screw who would not see reason. Joe Martin was within hearing distance of the argument and Ron did not want to get him involved. He called Joe into one of the cells and said, "I'm going to do that bastard. You stay out of it, Joe, and wait here till it's all over."

But Joe answered, "No, I'll make one with you, Ron, in case the rest of the screws get heavy."

Ron replied, "No, Joe, do it my way. I know what I'm doing. You just wait there and when you hear the bell go off, take no notice. I'll just let them take me to the block when it's over." Ron was referring to the chokey block where one is taken after any trouble and where you get locked up for twenty-three hours out of every twenty-four.

Ron then walked away from Joe in the cell, went right up to the screw he had been arguing with and hit him with a right-hand punch to the cheekbone. The screw went over on the floor, and another screw, who had seen this, rang the alarm bell. Ron just stood there, waited for the screws to gather round him and said, "Perhaps I'll get my medication now. Take me to the block." They grabbed Ron by the arms and took him to the chokey block where he was given fifty-six days in solitary confinement.

It was later discovered that the screw Ron assaulted had a broken cheekbone. If this had been known at the time, Ron would have got more punishment. News of the assault and the sentence for it was broadcast on the radio.

By now, we were getting used to living in prison cells. They are not luxury flats. They are bare and sterile. We have to use plastic cutlery and plastic chamber pots. Some cells have compressed cardboard furniture, in case of prisoners trying to smash things up out of frustration. I made my cell in Parkhurst comfortable. I had photographs adorning the walls, and I had a Chinese lantern. I named the cell "The Blue Lagoon".

Strange as it may seem, there's a lot of humour in prison. I once saw a con in Parkhurst so oblivious to his actions that he didn't realize how funny he looked. He was called Big John. He was a nice enough feller, about six feet three in height, with long hair down to his powerful shoulders and a long beard. He had cracked up on a couple of occasions, and on this particular morning, while we were getting ready to get our breakfast at the hotplate (on the ground floor where John's cell was), the word went quickly round that Big John had cracked up again. On my way to breakfast, I saw the giant figure of Big John with a mop in his hand, doing his best to stem a gush of water which was pouring from the taps he had left on in the bathroom. He was so intent on the job at hand that he didn't see the other cons walking by or the amazed looks he was getting as they ducked round him to get their breakfast. It was a humorous sight, even if sad.

I have met all kinds of cons in my time, including the famous bed-springs swallower at Parkhurst. The doctors had to keep operating on his stomach to retrieve them. He was eventually certified and sent to Broadmoor. I was, at one time, quite friendly towards him.

This same feller once had the needle with his brother who happened to have a beautiful garden. So the swallower of bed-springs got in touch with the police and told them he had buried a body in his brother's garden. Because the bed-springs man was in for murder and was a bit of a nutcase, the police dug up the whole garden with all its beautiful rose trees looking for the body. Alas, there was no body, but when the spring-man heard the good news of the upturned garden, he was overjoyed and decided the police were his best friends.

Another character I liked in the prison hospital at this time was Ron Abrahams who was named the "Screaming Skull". He was always furiously marching up and down a certain pathway in the hospital gardens, and if anyone should dare to encroach on the pathway at the same time, he would go into mad tantrums, wave his arms and scream abuse at the intruder. He also used to practise his own brand of yoga. I have, on occasion, had some cupfuls of hooch with him and found him to be a very interesting character, one of the old school.

I remember another nutcase who was walking around the garden path one day when he saw a little screw standing near the toilets. The nutcase walked up to the screw, hit him on the jaw, and the screw was on his arse. The alarm bell went, the screws got his arms up his back, and they said to him, "Why did you do that?" He replied, "I don't like midgets." He was hauled away to be placed in the strongbox until he cooled down.

Then there was the day I was walking round with my friend Mick Peterson, talking about nothing in particular, when I noticed him go livid white round his nostrils. He then walked away from me, marched straight up to the toilet door, and butted one of the windows in. He sat down as though relieved, and again the bell went. Mick, like the midget-hater, was dragged off for a rest period.

During my stay in the prison hospital, I was locked up for twenty-three hours a day, although I could have another hour in the TV room if I wanted. In this room, on the top floor, all the nutters would sit staring at the TV screen—that's if it wasn't being hurled to the ground with a crash. I used to sit on my own at a table to the left of the room and write letters.

During rest spells from letter-writing, I would take in everything I saw, and I saw some strange goings-on. Some of the unfortunate inmates who were sick or who didn't know a better way of life would scoop their plastic cups into the swill bucket beneath the tea urn, collecting the slops which they would then drink.

The patients in the hospital were in a worse state than those who had been certified and sent to Broadmoor, because they had yet to be assessed and so the medication they so badly needed had still not been sorted out.

I was sitting writing one night at the table when a small, slim Chinese feller came to my table. I noted that he was very agitated, and though he could hardly speak a word of English he kept repeating the same few words over and over again. They were, "CID fitted me, Soho." I nodded my head in agreement, which seemed to please him immensely, and we got on like a house on fire after that. I managed to communicate to him that at one time, I'd had a club in Gerrard Street, Soho—the El Morocco—and that I had Chinese friends in the East End of London. Every night after our first meeting, he would come to my table and spend ten minutes or so uttering the same words, "CID fitted me, Soho." I would continue to nod in assent.

I spent five Christmases in that part of the prison, and on each Christmas night, I would go to the toilet, which had a window overlooking miles of the Isle of Wight. I would peer out of the window and wonder what life went on amidst the twinkling lights I could see in the distance, and I thought to myself that any Christmas I spent differently to this would be a bonus.

I have known some cons who would literally do anything to get a shift from the hospital to better surroundings—even to the extent of planning the murder of any innocent party who would suit the occasion. I did not agree with this type of thing, and on the rare occasions where I knew of plans like these, I would let the plotters know I did not approve.

However, many of the violent acts committed in prison are not premeditated.

One of the most brutal attacks ever committed at Parkhurst was again in the hospital part, in the little garden area. A couple of inmates were sitting quietly on park-bench type of seats having a chat when the spring-swallower picked up half a house brick from the rockery garden, placed it behind his back, calmly walked up behind one of the two on the park bench and proceeded to smash his head in.

The alarm bell went and the spring-man was wrestled away from his victim, but the damage had been done. The poor feller

The Double 'R' Club

Ron and Billy
Daniels

Above: Pat Kennedy, Reg and two other publicans

Above right: Scotch Ian Barrie and Reg

Right: Big Pat Connolly, Archie Moore, Cowboy McCormack, and Ron

Reg and Christine Boyce

(l-r) Ron, Sammy Lederman, Joe Louis, and Mickey Morris

Right: Ron and Christine Keeler

Below: Tom Driberg, Frances and Reg, 1962

Ron, Ted 'Kid' Lewis and Sophie Tucker

Bobby Ramsey, Tommy Brown and Reg, 1963

(l-r) Reg, Eddie Pucci, Sam Lederman and Ron

Rocky Graciano and Ron

Brad Lane, Reg's adopted son

who had been attacked was reduced to a cabbage. His brain would no longer function. I was in a cell opposite to his. He was a sorrowful sight. He did not even know where he was.

I should point out that the spring-swallower, even with his bad record, was taken off the high-security-risk Category A years before I was, and he was shifted to a less secure prison, also years before me. I cannot figure out a system which allows this type of thing to happen.

There were three murders in Parkhurst during the time I was there. The first happened in the special unit of C Wing where I served some time. A con by the name of Dougie Wakefield lured Terry Peake, a lifer, to his cell and battered him senseless with a cosh, then strangled him to death.

Wakefield was already serving life for murder. For the murder of Peake, he was sentenced to life again. He had previously killed his uncle in the same way that he killed Peake. Terry Peake used to cut my hair, and he was very good at art, especially portraits. He was quite a likeable feller.

The second murder was when Johnny Patton stabbed to death a con by the name of Magee. Magee was lining up getting his breakfast when Patton came up behind him and plunged a knife in his back. Magee fell to the floor fatally wounded. The cons in the queue were rather callous—they just stepped over Magee and continued to organize their breakfast. It seems that Patton and Magee, who were friends, had had an argument the previous night over something or other, and the result was the death of Magee. Patton, who I always got on well with, was already serving life, same as Wakefield, and he also received a second life sentence. The last I heard of him, he was being kept in the cage in solitary confinement for an indefinite period at Wakefield Prison.

The third murder was towards the end of my stay at Parkhurst, in 1986, when a nutter plunged a long knife into a decent friend of ours called Rocky Harty. He was working in the kitchen at the time.

Unlike many of the cons in the prison, I eventually learned to be very tolerant towards my fellow inmates. It's a natural part of maturing that one learns to reason things out better. I like to try to deal with confrontation by taking the object of the argument away. It's not worth retaliating. I find, too, that it helps me a great deal if I choose my friends in prison very carefully. If one was to take offence every time one came across an ignorant con in prison, one would end up committing murder, or at least being certified insane.

Ron was certified a paranoid schizophrenic in 1979 and transferred to Broadmoor. Before he left, he met another con there, Joe Reading, who was an old friend of our father. He told Ron he had cancer. He said, "Seeing as I don't have long to live, is there anybody you would like me to kill?" Ron told him no, there wasn't. Poor old Joe went out and died a month later. I like to think that he's in a better place now, God bless him.

In 1980, I went to Long Lartin prison for eighteen months, and succumbed to a long attack of paranoia, an illness which convinced me that my family and I were friendless. I was not even troubling to shave or comb my hair, and I had stopped answering my letters which were piled up in the corner of my untidy cell.

One day I switched on the radio in my cell and I heard that Barry Manilow, the singer, was flying into the country, that he was due to touch down at London Airport and that there was a crowd waiting to greet him. In my confused state of mind, I thought it was myself they were waiting for at the airport, so I had a shave, got ready for the journey and waited. After some time had elapsed, I rang the bell on my cell door and a little while later a screw opened it. He said, "Yes? What do you want?" I said, "What time are we leaving?" The screw looked at me with a puzzled expression. And here I am all these years later, still waiting to go to London Airport. . . .

The problems with my illness worsened and, when I was sent back to the hospital at Parkhurst, I attempted suicide. I tried to slash my wrist with a broken piece of glass from my TV spectacles. I was doing this for my family's sake. My state of paranoia made me feel for no clear reason that we had no friends and that I was responsible for this situation.

It was suggested at the time that I cut my wrist so as to get to Broadmoor with Ron. This was completely against the grain, and my principles. Admittedly, I was ill at the time. But I would not have liked to have had my head doubted in any way, and I have never had any desire to go to Broadmoor or any other mental institution. Though I am physically a captive, I get enormous pleasure out of the fact that my thoughts are free.

My recovery began when one day I had a visit from a friend, Fred Bone. He left me a book, the autobiography of Meyer Lansky, the Mafia boss who was famous for his financial genius. I felt too ill to read much, but I did pick the book up a few times for a glance through its pages. I admired Lansky as a man, and each time I glanced at the book, the theme of his story seemed to be like a personal message to me. His life's philosophy was that one should never give up, even in the face of almost impossible odds. Lansky was only a small man in size, but he was powerful in stature, and he was afraid of no one. I eventually got engrossed in the book, and have never looked back since. When I completed it, I felt much better, and I was determined that Lansky's philosophy was going to be mine, so that I would also battle against the odds.

The same day I finished the story, I removed a four- or five-day growth of beard, had a shower, combed my hair and started to sort out all the unanswered mail. I replied to each one, and I have not stopped writing since that day.

It's ironic that Meyer Lansky had the control of the Colony Club in London and that, in the Sixties, Ron and I used to get a pension from this same club. Perhaps the fact that Lansky and I were in a way distant allies made his philosophy more influential than any talk by a doctor would have been. It seems that the ghost of the late Meyer Lansky had reached out to help me in my hour of need.

I did a lot of self-analysis on my recovery from this bout of illness, and studied subjects such as positive mental attitude, which I discussed from time to time with Charlie Richardson while he was in Parkhurst.

To digress for a moment, I would like to make it quite clear that Ron and I are the best of friends with the Richardson brothers and Frankie Fraser, names which are famous for being at one time the Krays' biggest enemies. Frankie Fraser and I were in different parts of Parkhurst at the same time and for many years, Frank, Ron and I kept up communication by sending messages via the prison grapevine. My brother Charlie, Frank Fraser and the Richardsons met socially recently, and I would like to take this opportunity to thank them for being good friends from a distance.

Returning to the subject of my experience of paranoia, I should add that it did result in enabling me to understand more of how Ron was feeling when he was going through bad patches in his illness. While he was in Parkhurst, Ron had two lots of electric shock treatment, administered by the head doctor. He wasn't worried about it beforehand. He was laid on a hospital table and given an injection to knock him unconscious. When he woke up, it was all over. He could smell the stuff they had injected him with, and he lost his memory for a few hours, but that gradually came back. They gave him a cup of tea, and he told me he felt calmer and not so muddled in his thoughts. It did him a lot of good.

Both Ron and I have learned a lot from prison. For instance, it has taught me the virtues of patience and self-discipline. When I was a smoker during this sentence, I used to split matches with a needle. I would do boxes of them, to promote my patience and also to be conservative with my meagre canteen wages.

This contrasts sharply with my earlier ideas of patience. When I was about sixteen years of age, a villain slighted someone very close to me during a party one night. This villain belonged to a firm, so I vowed I would wait and get revenge. Fourteen years later, I was at a drinking party with him. He had had a few, so I deliberately set out to provoke him in a heated conversation. He fell for the trap, and had a go at me verbally, whereupon I hit him on the chin with a right hook which knocked him out and broke his jaw. To this day, that particular villain doesn't know I waited fourteen years for my moment. As I said, that's patience of another kind. . . .

I lost my patience completely another time I broke someone's jaw. I was in the Green Dragon Social Club which was run by a feller called Sonny the Yank. He had been on Jack Spot's firm at one time. I had been having a drink with him and another man and I was putting my overcoat and kid gloves on ready to leave when the Yank called me "son" in what I felt was an insulting manner. So I hit Sonny the Yank on the point of the chin with a right hook that lifted him three feet into the air. As he was falling, I grabbed him by the shirt collar and butted him in the face, but it was not necessary. The first punch had knocked him out cold. I later discovered I had broken his jaw.

The next night, we heard that there had been a shooting incident at the Pen Club in Spitalfields Market. One of the owners, Jimmy Cooney, had been shot dead in an argument with some customers. The other, Billy Ambrose, had been shot in the stomach. He drove himself to the London Hospital.

I went to see Billy Ambrose in the hospital, and while I was there, I saw Sonny the Yank on the opposite side of the same ward, three beds away, lying there with his jaw wide open. . . .

Those were violent days; they seemed worlds away from my existence at Parkhurst Prison. But our friends from those times had not forgotten Ron and me.

The mail arrived one day, and amongst my three or four letters was one with a Bayswater postmark. It was from our old friend Billy Hill, the boss of London, now returned from Tangier. He was about seventy years of age by this time, and he had written a touching letter. I had just missed being able to shake hands with him at my mother's funeral in August 1982, because the seating arrangements weren't quite what we'd hoped. The letter said that if he could do some of our time for me and Ron, he willingly would. Sadly enough, Bill passed away two years later.

The death of our mother was a devastating blow to Ron and me. Ron has written several poems in an attempt to express his grief and loss, and some of the lines are almost unbearably tender: "So go to sleep, Mum, I know that you are tired. . . ."

Sorrow is a subject that I have unfortunately come to know a great deal about, having lost my wife Frances, then my mother and then after that my father. But I have learned that sorrow is the sister to happiness. They rock like a seesaw in life. At times we are all sad, we all meet sorrow and adversity, but it is best that we do not let it weigh down that end of the seesaw. Of course, if we love and lose someone we feel and show sorrow, but those we lose would wish to see the ones they left behind happy.

There was chaos when Ron and I were released from prison, in handcuffs, for our mother's funeral service. We saw crowds of onlookers and press and media people as well as our own family and friends who had come to pay their genuine respects. Ron was the first person to be given permission to leave Broadmoor for a funeral. He would also become the first person to have a wedding inside the hospital in 1986 when he married his first wife, Elaine.

We decided that it would not be what my father wanted for us to attend his funeral, too, with all the attendant fuss. His burial was a comparatively quiet event. I knew he had died before I was told. My friend Fred Bone came on a visit to tell me, and I already knew, somehow, what he was going to say before he spoke his chosen, hurried words. He said, "How come you are not surprised?" I was at this time too overcome with emotion to explain to him.

They say that twins have psychic powers which enable one to know what the other is thinking, even from a great distance, and I have found this to be true over the years. Ron and I can pick up on each other's moods. One time, we sent each other letters which crossed in the post. We each revealed to the other that we were going to buy a budgie and a cage. This is just one of many instances where we have had similar or the same thoughts across the miles.

I have known times where I have been psychic with other people and read their thoughts. On one particular occasion, just before midnight, a mini-cab picked us up at Vallance Road to take us to the Stork Club, off Regent Street. I sat behind the driver and had the urge to tell him something of his past and of his future. I stared intently into the back of his neck, and concentrated my thoughts on him. I could see he was starting to get uncomfortable, but I continued to stare and concentrate. Then I spoke from behind him. I said, "I feel that you've spent some time in Australia recently, and that your ambition is to be a writer of short stories. But you have not been encouraged in this by your wife and so you are thinking of becoming a teacher." I also added, "Continue with your writing. It will lead you to happiness."

The driver almost broke his neck turning round towards me in amazement. He said, "How do you know these things? I've never told anyone about my writing. A year ago, I came back from Australia to start this job, and I was also thinking of becoming a teacher." We reached the Stork Club and the doorman came to the cab to greet us. I went to pay the driver and he was shaking, refusing to take the money. The way I had been concentrating on the feller's past and future had drained me dry, but I soon put that right with a few gin and tonics when I entered the club.

A couple of days later, the cab driver again came to Vallance Road. He brought a stack of his short stories for me to peruse. It took some time for me to convince him I had not been spying about his past. Perhaps it was the gypsy in me that enabled me to read him the way I did.

On another occasion, in Parkhurst Hospital, I picked up the bad vibes of a feller in the next door cell to me, even through the thickness of the concrete wall that separated us. I knew he was paranoid and having bad thoughts about me. The following morning, when both our cell doors opened, I walked into his cell and confronted him in a gentle manner. I asked him why he had had bad thoughts about me. He broke down and admitted that it was true, and I did everything I could to put him at his ease, knowing he was ill.

There was an odd experience once when we were locked up for about three hours so that the screws could have a cell search. Just before we were unlocked, I suddenly knew that out of 200 cons, one of them had a knife hidden, and I knew, inexplicably, the landing and location of his cell. I later found out that I was correct about all of this, including the knife. Something else I knew, by some very strange psychic instinct, was that the man intended to use the knife on me. He later confirmed this in a conversation with someone else.

There are other, more recent, examples of this ability to foresee things. Not long ago, in Lewes Prison where I still am today, I was standing outside the screws' office, which was empty, when the phone in the office started to ring. I knew without any doubt that it was my friend Pete Gillett on the phone with a message for me. I was so sure of this that I beckoned to a screw on the landing above to come down and answer the phone. My friends Tony and Dougie, who were with me, can bear witness to this.

Dougie at the time was having bad problems outside, and although I did not know what they were about, I had a vision of a woman who was causing problems by gossiping. I described this woman to Dougie who confirmed that it fitted the description of his mother-in-law and that she was indeed the cause of all his problems.

I have also had some experience of the power of thought. On 27 November 1985 at 4.35 pm, I was in my cell in Parkhurst, relaxing. There was a tap at the cell door, and the little spyhole was opened from the outside. I walked to the door and peered through. Bernie Glennon, a very good friend of mine and a fellow lifer, was outside. He spoke in a quiet voice and said, "Under the door, Reg." There appeared on the floor half a page of foolscap paper. The written message said, "Reg, Eddie Kelly has just been taken over to the hospital on a stretcher, unconscious."

Eddie Kelly was twenty-six years of age and serving a fourteen-year sentence for armed bank robbery. A married man with an eight-year-old son, he had started the sentence at the tender age of nineteen. I had had the pleasure of meeting his wife and son during visiting times. She is one of the nicest people I have come across, and the boy is a smashing kid.

I had known Eddie for about five years, and my first reaction on reading the message was to be emotional and very concerned for him. I was baffled, too, because only that morning I had seen and spoken to Eddie and he had seemed fit and well.

I decided to ring the bell which would summon one of the staff to my door. Someone eventually appeared, and I said I wanted to know how Eddie Kelly was. He answered, "All I can tell you is that he was taken to the hospital unconscious."

I continued to pace up and down my cell, and then decided to ring the bell again. When the member of staff appeared for the second time, I asked him if it was possible to unlock me so that I could make further inquiries at the office below on the ground floor. He answered politely that I would have to wait until 6 pm when we would all be unlocked. I said a short prayer for Eddie's recovery. I knew that he would be under observation on F2 landing in the prison hospital. I psyched myself up and tried to direct my spiritual thoughts, willing Eddie to derive energy from the force I was trying to generate.

During this period of time, I could feel that he was slipping back into unconsciousness against his will so while pacing the floor, I did so in an aggressive manner and with clenched fists. I was also speaking aloud, "Come on, Eddie, wake up, stop slipping back, wake up." I continued this for a few minutes, and just before 6 pm, I had a feeling of well-being and knew that Eddie would be OK.

When the door was unlocked, I went to the office and spoke to the senior officer who phoned the hospital to find out about Eddie. He told me he had fully recovered.

The following day, Eddie was admitted back to the wing, fit and well. He had been suffering from some form of acute flu virus which had rendered him unconscious. Out of interest I asked if he could remember what time he had recovered consciousness. He told me six o'clock. . . .

I am convinced that with my genuine concern, I had generated some form of energy which roused Eddie, and that my prayers had been answered. I do not profess to be a spiritual healer or have some infallible psychic power—this was the first experience I had had of generating this form of faith healing from a long distance. I sincerely believe that on this particular night, I became a vehicle, and the energy I was trying to relay stemmed from my prayers.

I made various friends in Parkhurst who would tell me of their spiritual beliefs and goals. My interest in philosophy, religious and otherwise, goes back to my boyhood friendship with Rev. R. N. Hetherington. He was one of the best public speakers I ever heard, with a very powerful and clear voice. No one could fall asleep in the pews of his church. He spent a lifetime helping others and caring little for himself. He was always there if any of our family needed help and we, in return, would always be ready to assist with any of the church events he organized in Bethnal Green. As an adult, I listened for hours to his philosophies, and continued to visit him regularly when he moved to his small vicarage in Ealing. Today, our philosophies may be closer than they were back in those days. I cannot say I have come a very long way, but I would like him to know that I'm still trying.

Ron and I got to know the padre at Parkhurst Prison, Hugh Searle, quite well, and I am pleased to be able to count him amongst my friends.

I also struck up a friendship with a Buddhist monk called Bhante. He used to visit various cons in Parkhurst, and I would have long discussions with him while we shared a jug of mint tea. He came to see me every two weeks for some time, and at the end of our talks, I would always ask him to give me a little advice before he departed. It gave me food for thought during the long hours after 9 pm when I was locked up. I always felt a little wiser after talking to him.

People like these were a comfort to me after my illness and the death of my parents, as was another con called Steve Tully who was my best friend at that time. He helped me through a period when I found it difficult to settle down.

I also started feeling better after being moved from the hospital wing to the main wing in Parkhurst, once I got used to being in contact with many people again. I was able to feel happy in my surroundings, and to enjoy each day, not wishing the time away. The pen became the instrument of my emotions.

I compiled my *Slang* book with Steve Tully, and I became a very prolific writer, both in my personal efforts and in letters to my many penfriends across the country. I did a bit of painting, too. I felt stronger, having conquered the bad experiences of the recent past, and happy that I had friends around me.

When Steve left the prison, he helped me to organize charity shows outside. For my part, I tended to keep myself to myself a lot more, although I would still mix socially: you need to keep a balance.

And then, in December 1985, a young man of twenty-five years came into Parkhurst. He had been transferred from Coldingley Prison in Bisley, and he was serving six years for conspiracy to rob. Pete Gillett arrived at Parkhurst handcuffed to a screw and escorted by two others. He stopped at the gate, jutted his jaw out and said, "I made it, Ma!", splaying out his arms à la James Cagney in *White Heat*.

I met him the day of his arrival, and we greeted each other with a smile and a warm handshake. We got on just like old friends from the beginning. I found Pete to have a marvellous personality and sense of humour. He was born in Crawley, Sussex, and was a clean-cut type of person with exceptionally good looks. I soon learned he was extremely talented. He had won three disco-dancing medals, had a smashing voice and a wide repertoire of impersonations. He was a fantastic dancer.

Pete became my best friend at Parkhurst. We shared a lot of adversity as well as good times. It may be strange to think of having good times in a place like Parkhurst Prison, but we would have several friends join us in my cell and Pete would keep us all happy with his singing and dancing—something of a feat considering that prisoners are the hardest people in the world to please. Our friends often said that when Pete entertained, they would forget they were in prison for those few hours. He was so full of charisma that it overcame the sterile reality of the prison world.

When Pete was in Coldingley Prison, he had had a fight with a bully much bigger than himself. Pete really belted this feller, but during the fight, he went up against the wall. A nail that was sticking out from the wall went into his shoulder and left a scar. On hot days when Pete would be sunbathing, people would often say, "How did you get that scar?" And Pete would reply, "Reggie Kray did it." We met each other for the first time six months later!

Early in 1986, Pete persuaded me to stop smoking. I had been a chain-smoker for thirty-four years, but I have not had a cigarette since 1 February of that year.

For some time, I had been into positive thinking, and this helped me to keep my non-smoking promise to Pete. The first three days were the worst, but I found eating Polo mints very helpful. I found I enjoyed my meals more because I could taste the difference in my food, and my sense of smell improved, too. I noticed how powerful the stale smell of tobacco becomes to a non-smoker, and I now sympathize with all my old friends who must have found my habit very offensive.

Now feeling fit and healthy and on top of things again, I kept myself busy in the prison. I sent copies of *Slang* to Ronald Reagan, because I always believed in reaching high, and on the same day, I sent one to the Queen Mother. I'm a big fan of hers.

I went into the office and I spoke to the screw who sent out the parcels in a serious manner, even though I was joking. I said, "Make sure you write these two addresses on my record sheet in case any of you get any ideas of fucking me about." And I pointed to the addresses of Buckingham Palace and the White House in Washington! But the joke was on me, because some time later in 1986, I was sent to Wandsworth Prison on a lay-down, which is called a 10.74, and I was banged up for twenty-three hours a day for two months, so my connections didn't seem to help me! I had over 1,000 addresses on my record sheet at Parkhurst, but I was told it got lost when I was at Wandsworth.

I spent one month of the lay-down at Wandsworth and the next at Wormwood Scrubs. The 10.74 order says the inmate will remain at his destination prison for a designated period of time for an act against the prison system. There is no defence against this order, whether you are innocent or not.

On my arrival at Wandsworth, I was surrounded by six to eight screws and the one in charge said to me, "Which way are you going to have it while you are here? The easy way or the hard way?" They probably thought they were being brave, with the odds of about eight to one. I gave an answer which was neither too aggressive nor too submissive. I said, "The faster I get out of this dump the better."

During the same stay, I was having a shave in my cell one freezing cold day, stripped to the waist with my face all lathered up, when I was told by a member of staff that the reception screw wanted to see me along the corridor. I walked along there with the foam still on my face and the towel in my hand and met a six-foot screw who had an arrogant look on his face. He had an arrogant manner to match. He said to me, "I am checking a list of the stuff you brought with you from Parkhurst." He showed me the list, which I signed, and as I went to walk away to complete the shave and get the soap off my face, he called me back and said he wanted to recheck the list. I knew this was a deliberate act of hostility, because he then said, "Have you any false teeth for me to put on the list?" And he went on to ask a lot of other stupid questions. But I was ready for this rude person and refused to react to his hostility, which clearly upset his peanut brain. I pretended to be pleased to get out of my cell for a while, knowing that he wanted to annoy me by keeping me out in the cold. I went further; I started to suggest to the blockhead that there might be items on my record sheet he had forgotten to ask about, and in the end, he told me to go back to my cell. Of course, not all confrontations between staff and inmates end as peacefully as this one did. It's understandable that some cons do burn with fury and indignation, and eventually become bitter, when they are regularly subjected to such taunts from screws.

All I could see from my cell in Wandsworth was a damp, bleak wall. I had nothing to do for all those hours every day except listen to the radio and think my thoughts. I heard a news bulletin stating that in South Africa detainees were locked up for twenty-three hours a day. Here I was in the middle of London in the same situation and nobody could care less. Yet, I had served eighteen years of my sentence. I was not even allowed to exercise with anyone in the hour delegated for my walk in a wire cage.

I had another month of this at Wormwood Scrubs, although they were a lot more liberal there. They allowed me to walk in the exercise cage with an old friend of mine, Joe the Greek, who was also on a lay-down in the chokey block. The 10.74 people were made to stay at the back of the church on Sundays, segregated from the other prisoners.

But during such times of loneliness, it was amazing how a nod of the head or a hand wave from someone else gave one comfort. I had a much better view from my cell in the Scrubs. I could see the exercise area. I would watch the remands walking around in circles while I clung like a monkey at the window, watching. When someone I knew would wave to me, it made the effort of clinging to the window worthwhile. I was so close to friends, yet so far away.

During the Wandsworth month, I had a visit from the singer Roger Daltrey who came along with my brother Charlie. Roger said I should have it published in the newspapers that I was being locked up like an animal alone for twenty-three hours a day. But I didn't want to make trouble for myself or anybody else because I wanted to get back to Parkhurst as quickly as possible. I plagued the assistant governors in Wandsworth and the Scrubs about this.

There was a strike on in Parkhurst which had erupted into violence, and to make matters worse, the "burglars"—our name for security screws—had found a highly dangerous firebomb in the corner of Pete's cell. He hadn't known it was there. The screws had taken Pete and the bomb to a safe area and had put a match to it to demonstrate to Pete how dangerous it was. It was so inflammable that the bomb went up in fierce, scorching flames within a second of the match striking.

At the same time, our friend Rocky had just been murdered.

So having read about that in the newspapers, and hearing in letters from Pete about the strike and the firebomb, I was very concerned for Pete's safety.

Eventually, I was reunited with him and relieved to be back to the familiarity of Parkhurst where my friends were. I didn't spend a huge amount of my time with the cons outside of my own close circle, but I got on well with nearly everyone, including some terrorists who I was pleased to call friends. It's my nature, just as it is Ron's, to welcome foreigners to this country.

There was one foreign terrorist at Parkhurst who was serving life for assassination. He always refused to sign his name, in particular to documents or letters. Yet, one Christmas, out of respect to Ron and me, he made the kind gesture of sending Ron a Christmas card, and signed his name.

Some of the screws in Parkhurst were decent enough fellers, too. I used to like Mr Brooks who was one of the staff in the hospital. He was a karate expert, and a gentle giant of a man with a really good physique. He was always kind to the inmates, and I never, ever saw him take a liberty. He was helpful on keep-fit tips, and we got on well because we were both basically sportsmen. His wife was a nurse, and I used to give him the 300 to 400 Christmas cards I received each year so that she could pass them on to the children to play with.

I never came across any corrupt screws in all my years in Parkhurst, despite reports in other books that I bribed some of them. I also strenuously deny having ever said that cannabis or hooch is plentiful in prison, a remark which has been wrongly attributed to me. In any large establishment, there is always some small opening for illegal contraband, but I certainly never saw any large amounts of it.

The mid eighties were essentially happy years for me at Parkhurst. And then late one night, in January 1987, I was told without any warning that I was moving. The next day.

CHAPTER 7

FAITH, HOPE AND CAPTIVITY

On arrival at HMP Gartree, near Market Harborough in Leicestershire, I accidentally discovered that the screws are given soft toilet paper, while the cons have to make do with rolls which have the texture of sandpaper. I thought to myself that even in this dump there was class distinction.

It was a desolate place, Gartree, and I no longer had the company of Pete to brighten my day, but I settled into the routine after a fashion.

Each morning at 7.20 am, they would test the alarm bells as a signal that it would soon be time to rise. I would go for a shower as soon as my cell was unlocked, and it was like being in solitary confinement. I would usually be alone in the shower room because the other cons on this manor were reluctant to step under the water. They shied away from the showers as though they were out of bounds, or they were afraid they would drown!

There were a large number of rapists and child-killers in Gartree. I believe one can get the tick and pulse of the streets by looking around in our prisons, and this one certainly served as an indication of what the cities, towns and even villages are like today, with rampant rape and child killings. This is a sad reflection on society, and when I think of the fighting men I knew in the past, I yearn for yesterday and the principles that went with it.

I remember seeing cons in Gartree showing out to the rapists. Perhaps they did this to keep themselves in the clear in the event of anything happening to the rapists, although it's unlikely that much would happen to a rapist in today's prison society. Unfortunately it is becoming normal for them to be integrated. I once saw a screw giving extra potatoes to a rapist. I guess the screw wanted to build him up for the next time he rapes someone. Sometimes the system seems so unfair: no rapist ever did twenty-one years in dispersal prisons, but I did.

My job at Gartree took about twenty minutes or less, twice a day. Four or five other cons and I would pull a large barrow around the grounds and pick up the rubbish which had been left out in plastic bags. In the summer we would wear shorts and boots or trainers. Near the hospital part, there were some beautiful flowers of all kinds and colours, which reminded me of my mother. She loved flowers. They also reminded me of a saying I once read in a book that "flowers are God smiling at us".

I would go to the gym for an hour each day, and I would also spend quite a bit of time answering my mail, which is censored before I receive it. People from all over the country write to Ron and me. They seem to relate to us in our adversity. Many of these people are suffering in some way themselves, so they see Ron and me as allies. I get about twenty letters a day, and I usually manage to reply to all of them. Sometimes I wish I was a typewriter! Nearly all of the people who write to me are supporters who say that Ron and I should be released, and that I am welcome at their homes when I get out of prison. Each letter tells me a different story of the outside, so I can never be bored. My greatest pleasure is in writing letters to my close friends, in other prisons and outside, and Ron and I write to each other at least once a day. A lot of the letters I write are serious, but I like to have fun with them, too. I recently ended a letter to a young friend of mine by telling him that I had to go because the milkman was at the door and the dog was barking!

In other spare hours in those early days at Gartree, I would read, listen to the radio and play LPs on the record player in my cell, so I was always busy, even though I spent practically all the time in my own company. All I needed was the stimulation of good thoughts, with music as my atmosphere.

Many of the other cons spent their time in the TV room, regardless of what was on. They seemed to be oblivious to the reality of this grey world of prison. Ron and I have never been avid TV fans. We watch the news, but we're very selective about everything else. Ron enjoys wildlife programmes, Benny Hill and *Neighbours*—he was sorry when Kylie Minogue left because Charlene was his favourite character!—and I will watch documentaries and other informative programmes or TV specials.

Neither of us are *EastEnders* fans, although I was amused when my *Slang* book appeared in a recent episode. It just doesn't seem like the East End I knew. The dialogue has people saying things like, "There's a policeman." The real chat would have been, "There's an old bill over there" or "Look at that slag!"

Television is a propaganda machine, filtering out to the sheep-like audience whatever it wishes to tell them. It also helps to nullify unrest among everyone from prisoners to the unemployed. I was not cut out to be a spectator. I prefer to participate in life's activities, even if only to play a game of table tennis or snooker. I see a story wherever I go, so I do not need the television.

Gartree Prison itself was a desolate place. The view from my cell window reminded me of a scene from a film about a prisoner of war camp, especially when I would look out in the early hours and spot a screw walking round the grounds with an Alsatian dog.

Two or three days stand out from the others in the couple of years I spent there. One was the helicopter escape. From the wing window, I saw the helicopter land and John Kendall and Sid Draper clamber aboard to scarper off into the distance. After that, a whole series of helicopter jokes went around the prison. Somebody put a notice up on the board saying, "Authorized flights to and from Gartree. Tickets to be obtained at the office. Please check with security."

Following the escape, the prison authorities fitted wire cables across the top of the open exercise compound so that helicopters could not land. Small, orange-coloured balls were strung out across the cables. They looked quite pretty when I looked out of my cell window early each day. They reminded me of the fairground's lights at Victoria Park in the East End of London when I was just a kid.

Before the escape, we used to have exercise at a regular time. But after it, we would have exercise at odd times, to prevent any future escapes being planned so easily.

Another day, around 6.30 pm, the alarm bell went and the wings were sealed off because two teachers had been attacked and cut with a knife. It was said that there was an attempt by two young prisoners to take the teachers hostage, but they were overpowered and taken to the chokey block.

On another occasion, the alarm sounded when a feller called Mick Hallett smashed up the office in B Wing.

At one time, we could go on inter-wing association where we would stand outside the wing gates talking to friends. This was stopped when a couple of cons broke into the canteen and stole a quantity of tobacco. The authorities considered this the height of audacity. But I guess there were a lot of thieves about!

One morning, a feller slashed his arm in the cell opposite to mine. Fortunately, he was brought out alive.

Then there was the afternoon a screw brought snakes in for us to see and I handled a python. It reminded me of Read and Gerrard.

But apart from the incidents mentioned and the occasional fight, the prison ran smoothly and one day was pretty much like the next.

I started to enjoy myself more in April 1987 when Pete was released from prison. He visited me regularly, and still does, as my unofficially adopted son, and I gained great pleasure from being involved in the launch of his career as a singer and TV personality. I became Pete Gillett's gospel-spreader, writing to all of my penfriends to tell them about his record, *Homeless Child*, which was released on IRS in 1988, about his live shows in clubs around the country and about his TV appearances. Some of these were on programmes to do with Ron and me, but the biggest was in May 1988 when he was chosen to go on a survival week on an island off Sri Lanka with Annabel Croft, the ex-tennis player and TV presenter, actor Simon O'Brien who played Damon Grant in *Brookside*, and a merchant banker called James Vincent. Their adventures on the island were filmed and broadcast in weekly instalments on the TV programme *Network 7*. In my opinion, and the opinion of the producers, Pete was the star of the show, a natural in front of the camera.

By this time, I had started to socialize a bit more at Gartree. Harry Roberts, the cop killer, was there. He's the only con in the country who spent longer than me in the dispersal system. Joe the Greek was about to be transferred to Gartree, too. And I had become good friends with a likeable feller called Bernie Clewett. He was sixty years of age and had been sentenced to life imprisonment for the first crossbow killing, so he is in the record books. He is known as Bernie the Bolt.

My two best friends in the prison were Mick Bartley and Mick Archer. Mick Bartley was from just outside Durham. He was twenty-five years of age, intelligent, well built, good-looking and a man of top principles. He had done boxing and kick-fighting. He was, and still is, serving twelve years for robbing a security van of £100,000. He was convicted at the early age of twenty, and he was on his fifth year when I met him. We never had one argument in all the time we spent together in Gartree. The same can be said of my relationship with Mick Archer who comes from Nottingham. He too is a likeable personality with good principles. His sentence was eight years for robbery.

I would usually eat lunch in Mick Archer's cell, and Mick Bartley would join us.

It was in Gartree that I decided to write this book, and Mick

Archer was of invaluable assistance. Each day, in between work periods, we would sit down with cups of tea and I would dictate these stories while Mick wrote them down in longhand. Mick, at twenty-seven, enjoyed catching a glimpse of a past which has gone by far too quickly.

I look forward to the days when the two Micks and I will be on the street again to enjoy a few gin and tonics while we talk about the bad old days at Gartree.

It was during this period, in July 1988, that my Aunt May died. This took a lot out of me. I was very sad. She was the closest I had left apart from Ron and my cousin Rita. I took comfort at this time from thinking of my friends and of Pete, who to me is my family. My Aunt May had a good sense of humour. I know she would have laughed about her passing being mentioned by the media. Now I know she is still happy and she inspires me to go forward and to progress.

One thing which infuriated me, the same month, was an article in the *People*. It stated, "Soap superstar Leslie Grantham, Dirty Den in *EastEnders*, is the target of a sordid sex smear . . . Behind the sick campaign is brawny Paul Goodridge, minder to showbiz celebrities and self-confessed friend of the vicious Kray twins." He has not been a friend of ours for some time and certainly never will be again now that he has put Dirty Den through any hardship. We admire Dirty Den and are disposed towards him in a friendly way, even though we have not met him.

The autumn and winter of 1988 passed slowly and mostly uneventfully, apart from the publication of *Our Story*. I would look out at the snow touching the soil beneath my window and think how I would love to go for a walk on those cold, crispy mornings. But, alas, it was not to be. I recalled how I loved to walk the streets of the East End in the snow. It used to bring an unusual silence to the streets as people walked, the comforting silence of peace.

The Olympics started, my fifth Olympics away from London. This reminded me how long I'd been away. I felt as if I was in exile.

I shared my birthday dinner of turkey, ice cream and cake with six other cons.

There were more deaths, too. Our friend Jim Harris died in November, and the next month, the singer Roy Orbison passed away, which made me really sad. His is a tragic loss.

Christmas 1988 was a pretty miserable time. We had a lousy meal on Christmas Day, and no visits either that day or the next. I was allowed to send only twenty-four cards.

I was raring to get into the New Year when I expected to be released from maximum security. Then I could relax and enjoy my writing and my new interest in writing lyrics for pop songs. Pete had already recorded one song, *Masquerade*, using my lyrics and he has since recorded another, *I Began To Notice*. But following an article in *Melody Maker* in the autumn of 1988 about this new interest of mine, I began to receive enquiries from musicians I had never met. I had a visit from Nasty Suicide, formerly of the Scandinavian band Hanoi Rocks, and he has now recorded a demo tape which includes my lyrics on a song called *Retribution*, about the killing of Jack "The Hat". I have also had correspondence with a British group called Das Psycho Rangers, and with a singer called Buttz whose group is Last of the Teenage Idols.

I was very proud to be in *Melody Maker*. It was a new audience for me, and a favourite one, because music is the heartbeat of life. Who would be without the birds in the sky? Ever since I can remember, and especially in the club days, music has always been part of my background. We have had some big stars sing personally for us in clubs, and certain of these became good friends. I used to take my favourite records to all the parties in the sixties, everything from soul music to Shirley Bassey, Fats Domino to Elvis. The king Presley was the greatest. He truly was blessed with a voice.

Since I have been in prison, I have made friends with various contemporary musicians like Jools Holland, UB40 and Patsy Kensit. I'm godfather to James Kensit, Patsy's brother. I've also got an association with Spandau Ballet because of the

Kemp brothers Gary and Martin playing the parts of Ron and me in the film *The Krays*.

I like to keep up to date with all of today's groups. Whereas Ron likes to listen to classical music and opera, my preferences are for Bruce Springsteen, Dire Straits, Eric Clapton, Simple Minds and the Eagles. I also admire Jon Bon Jovi. He seems to have the right values regarding friends and family. He stood by his manager Doc McGhee when he was accused of smuggling cannabis into America. Jon Bon Jovi, though young in years, was mature in his generosity towards his older friend, and I figure that this kind of loyalty is his greatest character asset.

For twenty-two years I have had a constant companion sharing my cell with me, a great mate who sits on a chair close to my bed while I listen to his voice. He is my Murphy radio. My mother bought him for me in 1968 for £17. He is solid, with a good speaker, not like the plastic ones of today, and he is still as strong as ever in voice and body. He has been everywhere with me, he has been knocked about and covered in blood, one time my blood and the other time somebody else's, but he continues to hold up well. He is one of the old breed! He went missing for a few days once when I was taken to the chokey block in a hurry after having a row with someone, but he was returned to me eventually. I listen to Radio Two, Radio Four and, now that I am in the south of England, Capital Gold.

I watched *Live Aid* on television, and the Nelson Mandela birthday concert which was held at Wembley Stadium in June 1988. The fervour with which the huge crowd at the Mandela show showed their opposition to oppression of any kind warmed me to these beautiful young people, and made me proud to be British. It all reminded me in a way of the last night of the Proms, with its national spirit. Although there were many thousands at the concert, they were orderly and happy, in contrast to the football hooligans who get this country a bad name. The fact that it was viewed by billions was a massive boost for the young of this country.

The most affecting part for me was the sight of a beautiful

young person holding a white banner which proclaimed: "Hello to the TV room of Jesus." A simple truth.

Music keeps me company, music is my constant companion in my loneliness, music is my soul. In fact, I've got beyond the stage of loneliness. To be alone in these places is more of a pleasure than most of the other cons can give me. Their one topic of conversation is dirty drugs, which I find boring and limited. So I sit in my cell and listen to music and dream of the day that I might have some success as a lyricist. Naturally, I hope it will be Pete who gives me my first Number One single! How stimulating if one day our lyrics could be heard in the vast Wembley Stadium, with the kids joyfully tapping their feet and clicking their fingers to one of our songs, and recognizing us as songwriters—then these austere days spent alone would really bear fruit. One day I hope to have a glass of gin and tonic and share some laughter, happy that my present adversity fetched forth lyrics out of the silence, and that they are a success. Then I will drink a toast. Or two! Or three!

This gave me something to dream about as I entered the first weeks of 1989. There was good news for me, too: I was told I was going to be moved to a Category B prison for the first time since our arrests back in 1968. As the time for leaving Gartree drew nearer, I became fidgety and irritable because of the anxiety of waiting, but my heart was full of joy. The day I moved would be the day I'd take the first step towards my eventual release, and I wished my parents could be alive to see it. They, like Ron, helped me through twenty-one years in the dispersal system.

In February, I packed up all my stuff, including my curtains, and sent it to prison reception in readiness for the move. However, March came and went and there was still no definite date. First of all I was due to move in February, then March, and now they were talking about mid April. It was mental cruelty. All lifers are told well in advance when they are moving, and in twenty-one years of experience, I had never known a date of departure to be changed. I was the exception, yet I should have been out of the dispersal system years before.

Other lifers were being shifted without any delays or mishaps. I had heard of mind games being played with prisoners to see if they would snap or pass the distress barrier test, and I really felt they were pushing me too far. This sort of thing could only happen in *Porridge*, but I wasn't laughing.

Finally, it was confirmed that I would be leaving on 19 April. I reflected on my two years at Gartree. I guess the old place should take some credit—I did accomplish more on my writing there than anywhere else. There was so little social life I had to make my own, which was and is writing of past experiences to make up for the lack of them in the present. I also did some progressive thinking during my time in Leicestershire, which will stand me in good stead for the future.

The night before I left, Mr John Barton, the senior in charge of the wing, shook hands with me. I always found him to be helpful and reasonable. He was well respected by all on the wing, and there were always less problems when he was on duty.

My new home was going to be Lewes Prison in Sussex, just outside Brighton, and I couldn't get there quick enough, even if I did face the prospect of having to queue for a shower. I was looking forward to fresh pastures, and not having had a holiday in over twenty-one years, I was eagerly anticipating the more relaxed regime. I felt really high and buzzing and rejuvenated. Mick Bartley and Mick Archer both said I was acting like I was speeding. It was such a good feeling. I felt as though I was going home, now that the south once again beckoned me. It would be marvellous to be in my own territory after being in exile so long. I expected I would feel a little disorientated when I arrived, but it's all part of being a con. A new adventure awaited me. . . .

I arrived here at Lewes at 3.45 pm. As I had been told, it was very laid-back, and I christened it "Sleepy Lewes". A friend of mine, Ray Gilbert, came towards me to greet me, and I thought he was walking in slow motion. I was still speeding about as though I was in a dispersal prison, but soon I, too, was walking around quite slowly. In the past twenty-one years of my sentence, I had been nicked twenty-eight times, mostly for fighting and assault on screws, but that's because I was in the dispersal under pressure. Now I was out of it, I felt more settled.

I noticed that the place was full of mice. They were everywhere, sometimes even appearing at the height of activity and association time. But I had to laugh, because even the mice seemed to have the Lewes laid-back attitude. They seemed to amble about with not a care in the world.

It didn't take me long to adapt to the routine at my new prison, a routine which I'm still following today. Everything begins at 7.50 am when a handbell is rung. This is a regular sound throughout the day. It announces different stages in the prison routine, just as they used to do in the navy on board ship. I go right into the shower once the door is open, and after enjoying that, I slop out and tidy my cell. Then I go to the hot water urn to fill a flask for a cup of tea, and get my breakfast which could be beans and sausage, goulash or cornflakes, which we have twice a week. I also take vitamin pills, pollen B, kelp, alfalfa and yeast tablets. My mail will be censored and given to me by 9.30 am. I'm known as the "censor's nightmare" because I receive and send so much mail. The censor, Bert, often jokes with me about this.

I work as a cleaner, and between 9.30 am and 10 am, I see to a small area which has been designated to me to keep clean.

Lunch is served at 11.30 am. I usually have something like meat or stew with boiled potatoes and mushy peas. The food here is similar to what they serve in any institution, although Ron tells me Broadmoor food is good in comparison to most prisons.

We are locked in the cell between 12 noon and 1.10 pm. After that, I usually go to the gym for three-quarters of an hour. I go on the punchbag for four or five rounds, then do light weights and, finally, sit-ups. I will then have another shower, have a cup of tea and read some of my mail again.

We go on exercise in the small compound at 3.45 pm for forty-five minutes, take a walk or maybe just lie in the sunshine when it's hot. I hear the beauty of birdsong again at Lewes. I could never hear the birds whistling at Gartree because there were no trees nearby. I can see the rolling Downs in the distance, a beautiful sight. Lewes must be a lovely area. There is a small garden, and I noticed during my first summer that there were never any butterflies mingling amongst the flowers and lavender, although there were bees in abundance. I once read that to the bee, a flower is the fountain of life, and to the flower, the bee is a messenger of love. And both the flower and the bee gain real pleasure from each other, from the giving and receiving they take part in. I reckon everyone should become a member of Friends of the Earth and Greenpeace. We should attempt to remedy the environmental wrongs which pollute the atmosphere.

Tea is served at 4.30 pm, usually something light like bread and cheese with an apple. We are locked in our cells from 5 pm until 6.10 pm. Of an evening, I will have tea and a chat with my friends. Sometimes I wander round to other cells. Most cons are in pairs or small groups, which always reminds me of the film *The Odd Couple*.

There are table tennis, snooker and pool tables, a dartboard, a pretty large video room and televisions on each landing in the open, which I find is better than in a stuffy little room. The visiting room here is cosy and intimate with a counter for tea and coffee, soft drinks and confectionery.

There's a large football field for football and cricket. I've been playing football twice a week. The prison has a wing for young prisoners and also for those in remand, and there are education classes for art, etc. The remands are locked up almost twenty-three hours a day while awaiting trial, but the kids I've seen seem cheerful and able to cope well. I respect them. I do not see any depression or serious paranoia as I used to at Parkhurst and Gartree. Most of the Category B prisoners are at the end of their sentences.

I go to the Church of England chapel most Sundays. It's a pretty little place. The remands in the prison use the same church so there are always new faces to see and people to meet.

Also, people from outside occasionally visit the church for a social chat. Only recently, I met an American Christian lady in the church who came from Chicago, and I asked her if she was any relation to Al Capone!

I always bang up for the night at 8 pm. I usually go to sleep at about 9 pm, and I'm in such a good frame of mind, I need little sleep. I wake in the early hours, at about 3 am or 4 am, and catch up on my letter-writing. I cannot start on each new day quick enough.

My cell is large with big windows. It's painted in pale blue and white. I have a pale green bedspread, dark blue curtains and photos in gold and white frames all round the walls and on the table. There are photos of my late mother and father and my late wife Frances. Taking pride of place is my favourite photo—Frances and me in the Room At The Top in Ilford. She looks beautiful, as she was. There are other photographs, too, of Pete Gillett, his son Liam, my young pal Brad Lane, and other friends such as Barbara Windsor, Barbra Streisand, Diana Dors, Flanaghan and Jools Holland.

The crowd in Lewes are OK in general. One of the young lifers I respect is Patsy Dowling. He was given a life sentence for preventing three thugs from murdering his best friend. He accidentally killed one of the attackers. They say there are few greater loves than that of a friend for a friend.

There's a feller here called John Bates. He's a fellow lifer who was with me in Gartree. He is a typical Londoner and he has had hard times in the past, but has now levelled out. I often have a cup of tea with a few other inmates, Joe, a con from Belfast who is serving twelve years, and other friends called Danny Lawrence, Tony Scott and John Williams, a former legionnaire. There is a lot of potential talent in here. One feller is the greatest card man I've ever seen. He can do anything with a pack of cards, and is brilliant at telling fortunes with them, too. He can play any musical instrument, and is particularly talented with a guitar and harmonica. Another lifer, Eddie, is marvellous at reading palms.

One young feller, who has since left, was the most fantastic portrait painter I've ever seen. I particularly remember his attempts at a portrait of Lucien Freud, the great painter who was also a punter at my gambling club in Esmerelda's Barn.

I honestly believe this prison is a blessed place, not just because of all the talent within its walls, but because of its strange, relaxed atmosphere. They used to hang people here many years ago, and I do find it a spiritual environment. If the spirits of those who were hanged are still about, then I'm sure they are on my side, especially considering my feelings on capital punishment. I have looked at the gantry on the outer wall, the platform for the scenes of hanging in the old days, and I figure this place with all its history has more of a story to tell than an establishment like Gartree.

I feel Lewes is good for me. I seem to have got my head together, although I can still have the odd bad day, just like anyone. Sometimes I think to myself that as much as Lewes has a relaxed atmosphere and is in many ways a good jail, it is still a jail, and there's no place like the street. Just like a caged lion or tiger, I still yearn for freedom, though in a peculiar way. I might wake in the early hours and realize that all the street traders, who are my kind of people, would be getting ready to put the stalls out at Brick Lane and Petticoat Lane, just as I used to as a kid. I have to remind myself at times like this that locks, bars and keys do not make a prison as long as the mind is free to wander. At this stage in my sentence, there is no room for bitterness in my heart because in the past few years, I have had so much joy in discovering new friends and developing my own interests.

One day when I first came to Lewes, the welfare lady Judie asked me, "Don't you ever get fed up?" I replied, "Not often, I enjoy life too much." One can be just as happy in a desert as a hotel. It all depends on one's state of mind.

There are no real problems in life other than failing health. When one goes to a dentist or doctor for a check-up and is told there is nothing wrong, one feels a sense of relief and a new stimulation. All the world looks better. And that's purely because of one's state of mind.

It's been said by some that Ron and I sit in despair and have been unhappy ever since we were sentenced. I would like to put the record straight. These twenty-two years later, I feel fitter mentally and physically. I have kept myself in shape in every possible way, from my sessions in the gym to my morning routine of holding a towel and twisting it in alternate directions, from one end to the other, to strengthen my grip.

I believe that Ron and I have been blessed in many ways, particularly by good friends and fortune. This is all part of the philosophy which has helped me for the last two decades.

One of the things that we do wrong on the street is take life for granted too much. Being in prison gives one a new insight. If I were back on the street now, I would never take life for granted again. It's like the difference between swallowing food and chewing food. We all swallow life too fast and do not chew its pleasures. As the saying goes, what is life if we do not stop and stare?

Each day I say a prayer. It is not a prayer said in despair or sorrow, it is a prayer of thanks. I'm thankful for my friends and family, for being given the chance to live again through my writings despite the walls which have surrounded me, for being fortunate in my health when others are so tragically disabled, and for being given the ability to cope with my sentence.

I decided long ago that the best way to beat my sentence was to go along with the tide rather than swim against it and drown, to enjoy each day rather than wishing the time away. I cram as much into each day as possible because the more one puts in, the more one will get out of that day. If one watches a kettle boiling, it seems to take longer. My philosophy takes the watching of the kettle into consideration. Now, I find the days are going by far too quickly because I no longer wish my life away as I did during the first few years of my sentence.

Sometimes I get out of bed in the early hours to practise yoga, before starting work on my letter-writing. I suppose, at times, I am happier than others who may be sunbathing on Miami Beach or jetting round the world from one luxurious hotel to another. One may as well build castles in the sky as build dungeons below in one's thinking. It is just as easy to be optimistic in life as pessimistic. To an extent, it's true that we are a product of what we think we are. Worry has never solved any problems, bitterness destroys the one who is bitter, and the pessimist will always lack enthusiasm.

I have learned, over the years, to turn disadvantage to advantage, and although I cannot beat this sentence in terms of its physical length, I will have turned it to my advantage as regards the many friends and achievements I have made.

Money has always been secondary to me. A sense of achievement is what I strive for, and this has been an important factor in helping me to make the best of my predicament. Each day I give a little thought to my search for fulfilment. I strive to be someone in life—songwriter, poet, painter, I try them all. Maybe I have yet to find my true vocation. Hopefully I'll complete the search once I hit the street. I feel it will be something to do with helping other people in the fight against adversity. This would truly please me. To help someone is twofold joy. As they say, to give is to receive. It's the universal law that when one gives, it shall be returned. It's like the principles of love. It's complex, but there to be shared if we are lucky.

I believe that Ron and I were predestined to become known, either by fame or infamy. I seem to have walked a double path most of my life. Perhaps an extra step in one of those directions might have seen me celebrated rather than notorious. I always wanted to be recognized as the king of the clubs, but I chose the path I chose, so now I must walk it.

Why should I resent the hand which has been given to me? I will play it out to the best of my ability. The stakes have always been high. I have a lot of patience, and I hope luck is on my side so that I can continue to play a good game and end up a winner when I lay down my final card.

Even in moments of loneliness and depression, I will no longer give in to my difficulties. Like the true Scorpio I am, I will fight even harder when I know I am without the support of troops. It has helped me throughout my sentence to become indignant from time to time, because that is an energizing and strengthening emotion.

I have also drawn courage in my own situation from people who are in much greater adversity, yet show great bravery. There was a little boy by the name of Mario who was seven years old when the doctors said he did not have long to live. Yet he did not give up. He achieved his ambition of breaking the record for the biggest-ever number of get-well cards. He received thousands.

I'm still overwhelmed by the tragic story of a eleven-year-old English boy living in South Africa. James Fallon was just ten when he was knocked down by a fifteen-year-old joyrider. His skull was separated from his spine. He was left with a fully functioning brain but a body so paralyzed he could not even breathe or swallow without the help of machines. One of the most important involvements that Ron and I have had recently was our fund-raising campaign for the James Fallon Appeal. The most recent event was a boxing show in London.

In my daily prayer of thanks, I also pray for children like James, as well as asking that my friends be kept safe. I am a great believer in prayer, especially the positive thinking system of three-fold praying whereby one imagines a picture of what one is asking for. The three steps combined do bring results. It is not wrong to ask for what one wishes as long as one's plans also include others. Most of the great dreamers and thinkers throughout the world have been men of prayer.

I have kept my religious views a secret until now, because I did not want people to think this was a ruse to get out of the dispersal system or win parole. But now that I can see my freedom on the horizon, I can reveal that I became close to God in Parkhurst. I prayed for a friend who had cancer. This friend was cured in return for me being born again as a Christian. I could not and cannot become a saint overnight, but I leave it all in God's hands.

I know I can help many people; my notoriety will further this cause. Only a sinner would know the double paths of good and bad. The sanctimonious have not walked two paths. I have, and my paths have yet to lead to the ultimate one, so I have more to discover. I will be a vehicle of God. And what better vehicle than a one-time sinner who has shot four people and killed one of them? Born fighter . . . born again Christian.

I've already mentioned my ongoing interest in philosophy. I read all sorts of different books, my favourite being *The Prophet* by Kahlil Gibran. But I guess the closest we ever get to the answer of life is simply to enjoy it, because it is not everlasting in the physical sense.

Happiness whatever one's circumstances is not impossible to find, as I have said. For instance, watching Pete Gillett's progress since leaving prison has given me more joy than I could ever return.

I can think of two particular times at Parkhurst which drew me closer to him as family and friend. One was our first Christmas together. Pete and I and four others were about to begin our turkey dinner. Just as we were picking up the knives and forks, Pete interrupted and said, "I suggest that we say grace before we start the meal. Why don't you say it, Reg?"

I hesitated. I was a bit taken aback by his enthusiasm, especially in the presence of other criminals, and the sincerity of his request made me a little emotional. But I thought it was such a refreshing gesture that I agreed and did say grace.

The second event happened at 7.30 one morning when I took a cup of tea into Pete's cell. I was sitting on the end of the bed with the cups of tea in my hand and Pete was sitting up in bed singing a Mormon hymn. He was brought up a Mormon, but in later years changed to Church of England. Again, I was really taken aback. I shook my head in disbelief that I was seeing and hearing someone in Britain's toughest jail sitting in bed singing a hymn.

On the other side of the coin, there should be no doubting Pete's abilities as a street fighter. He can really use his hands and feet and head butts too in a fight. He also picked up the art of karate over the years. He's very physical. He is one of the best footballers I have ever seen, and is a qualified referee.

I consider Pete's son Liam to be a part of my family, too. He is ten years old as I write, and a lookalike of his dad with fair hair and blue eyes. When I saw Liam on a recent visit, he said he was proud of two people: his dad and me. This thrills me, coming from one so young, and inspires me to greater things. Liam is full of love, warmth and joy. I hope that one day he will be proud of Reg as an author.

In recent years, I brought three other young people into my circle of valued friends. One is Stephen Tully, Steve Tully's eleven-year-old son. I first met him when he came to visit his father and me at Parkhurst. He must have been about six at the time. All he knew of me was that I was, according to Steve, his grandfather. He looked up at me so innocently, and when his dad said to him, "Show Reg how you box," he closed his little fist and gently put it on my chin. I said to myself at the time, "How nice it would be if everyone could look at you with the eyes of a child."

Another of the children I brought into my family was James Fallon. I heard of his plight about a year ago, and became, over a distance of thousands of miles, very close to him.

His whole life was just a state of mind. He could only blink his eyelids or move his lips in some kind of sign language when he wished to convey something to his mother, father and sister. When he laughed, no sound came forth. When he cried, there were no tears. His parents only knew by the shutting of his eyes and his sorrowful look that he was crying. He had hopes, emotions and dreams. He prayed daily that God would make him better. He sent me a beautiful painting that he did with his mouth. Recently, ambulancemen took him and his wheelchair to a game reserve to let him see the elephants in their natural habitat. His mother Elaine sent me photographs of this joyful occasion. There was a baby elephant hovering above James, its trunk reaching towards him. James was smiling up at the elephant.

Sometimes when I hear people moaning and complaining, I say to them, "I had a little friend who would willingly have swapped all your problems and mine too for his." He was the epitome of courage, and it is with deep regret and sadness that

I have to tell you that he passed away on 21 March 1990. In the short time he was alive, he touched many hearts, just like a flower in spring. He will always have a place in my heart.

Last, but by no means least, is my adopted son, Bradley Paul Lane who lives in Doncaster, South Yorkshire. At the start of December 1988, he wrote and asked me for a signed photograph and told me all about himself. He enclosed a photograph of himself, along with a stamp. I did reply, and some time later, with the consent of his mother Kim, I adopted him. He is eleven and with his dark hair, he looks how I used to look at his age. He has a nice smile and brown eyes, cute and lovable. He is strangely like me when I was a child in other ways, too, even in the dialogue he uses. When I hear him talking or read his letters, it throws me back to my childhood days. He has brought such great joy into my life that I would not have altered my past steps because they led him into my family. Recently he sent me a signed photo which read, "To the best dad in the world from the best son . . ." I knew that once again I was blessed.

One of the things I have missed most over the years is the pleasure of young company, be it male or female. Young people stimulate my thoughts. I see them as people of song, each one bringing a new song as only the young can sing, musical as they flower in their youth. The kids of today are the light of the future. We should all take an interest in those whose society it will one day be. We should not be too busy to care.

I have an ambition, when I come out of prison, to start a home for young, destitute people. It's disgusting that so little help is available to these kids. I would make my home as luxurious as possible, finances permitting. I have already been offered the use of a country retreat near Birmingham, a monastery run by my friend Bhante, for holiday trips. I also have many youth club contacts who have pledged their help.

I feel that something more should be done, too, for young offenders. I think of the fellers on the coach, when I started my journey to Lewes. I just hope they will not end up serving as long in prison as I did. They were a good bunch, meant for better things.

I get angry when I get letters from young inmates in prisons, remand homes and similar establishments, telling me they wish for a better life. No help is given to them.

Just recently, I received letters from two new young friends in a remand centre in Leicester. Both have previous convictions and have been in trouble since they were children. Even now, they are just teenagers. Both wish to make improvements in their lives, but I know that when their cases come to court, they will receive fairly long sentences. There is so much good in these young people, but they will be given no guidance or advice, and no one will try to search out the talents of these youngsters so they can be cultivated as assets. Instead, they will languish in the strange society of the prison world and will be led into a sequence of events and experience that will take them directly into the criminal world.

It will become a way of life for them, just as my sentence has become a way of life for me. My contention is that more should be done for these young people who start out wrongly on the path of life.

It is so different in the United States of America where celebrities and public figures are encouraged to talk to teenagers who find themselves up against the law. The kids respect and listen to people who have made the grade, rather than the doddering old fools whose only wish is to preach.

I figure that many of these young offenders have just channelled their energies in the wrong directions because they did not see a choice. The mistake of their criminal offence should be turned to their advantage by those who know better showing them the right way.

When it comes to young offenders, thoughts, plans and actions should eventually replace the lock and key. We will only reap from society the seeds we plant.

I would also propose that practical help in the way of financial assistance should be offered to young prisoners upon their release to ensure that they do not become desperate enough to return to crime.

When I am eventually released, I intend to visit those in less fortunate circumstances than myself in prisons and institutions all over the country, to see if I can help these people in some way.

My advice to any young person, offender or not, would be to make something of your life, channel your energies into something positive. Most of us have a choice. People like my young friend James Fallan have not.

There are so many opportunities about today in careers, in everything from business to sport, screen and theatre. Strive to be successful and make your parents proud of you. You should not only think you are the best, you should know it, too, and then you ought to make it to the top of the mountain. If you should, by some chance, fail, at least you will be able to say that you ran a good race and enjoyed the run.

Sometimes it is difficult for kids to keep out of trouble, especially if you are like Ron and I were. But the best advice I can give is that you should join boxing clubs, where you will learn how to defend yourself should you need to, and youth clubs where you can play football and other types of sport, which will channel your energies into a positive area.

Don't take drugs. They only lead to peril. You don't need them. You should go through life with the personality God gave you. I do blame drugs for the increasing crime rate, especially in the juvenile age group. We must think like teenagers to be able to relate to these kids. They cannot be bullied. They must be coaxed. It is only when we begin to understand the kids that we have any chance of helping to solve the problem of drug abuse. We should find and encourage new avenues of joy, new stimulations.

My final piece of advice to young people would be on the subject of honesty. In all walks of life, there are acts of deceit and cheating. I suppose it can be said that the lower classes of the criminal element stick to robbing banks and security vans, whereas the upper class bracket steal money by fraud and deception. I do not advise that anyone be either of these criminal types, but when it comes to honesty, one should always be honest in the extreme with those close to you. One should never cheat one's neighbour. When we look in the mirror at the start of each day, it gives us a good feeling to know that we have a clear conscience. This may sound very presumptuous coming from Reg Kray, but my word has always been my bond. Which is more than I can say for some.

I'm reminded of the story of a traveller who stopped a wise man and asked him, "If you had a choice, would you choose a member of your family or your friend?" And the wise man answered, "A member of my family if he was more like my friend." I have some friends around me whose fierce loyalty is as close as any blood tie. Yet many of our actual family have let Ron and me down.

Our Aunt Rose's son Billy Wiltshire has never been to visit us. He didn't even attend our mother's funeral. He hasn't sent Ron a packet of fags the whole time we've been away. Many other relatives have been disloyal: Kevin Kray, who works down at Smithfield Meat Market, Billy Kray, Raymond Kray, Johnnie Kray and Freddie Kavanagh.

At the same time, many of our closest friends have been a tower of strength: Geraldine Charles, Charlie Smith (Ron's best friend in Broadmoor), our American friend Joe Pagano, Joe Martin, Tony McAvoy, Mick Peterson, Nicky Treeby, Jeff Allen, Billy Gentry, Harry "Hate 'Em All" Johnson, Len Maclean, Dave Hunt from Customs House, John Nielson, Brian Emmett, Dave Gannaway, Ken Stannard, Billy Knox, Les Berman, and many, many more.

I would especially like to mention my young friend Stephen Guttridge who is also serving time and has been exceptionally loyal to me over the years. He, too, loves writing. He sends me all his poetry, and is as close as close to me.

Ron and I have never forgotten the loyalty of those who did not turn traitor at the trial: our brother Charlie, Ian Barrie, Ron Bender, Tony and Chris Lambrianou and Freddie Foreman. Freddie was innocent of accessory after the fact to murder, but he got ten years for this and never once complained about it when I was with him in Leicester.

One day at Leicester Prison he did me a right favour. I had

an argument with a feller by the name of Peter Hurley in the little kitchen area, and I hit Hurley on the chin. He reached out for a knife, and Freddie Foreman placed his hand on Hurley's wrist to prevent him from picking it up.

Our celebrity friends have not forgotten us either. We have had visits and/or letters from all sorts of people, ranging from old friends like Barbara Windsor, Diana Dors and all of our boxing pals to newer acquaintances including the American singer Debbie Harry, keyboard wizard Rick Wakeman, Jimmy White, the snooker player, and Cliff Richard. When we were in Parkhurst, we had letters from the great fighter Joe Louis, all the way from Las Vegas, and the soul star Marvin Gaye, who was later shot dead by his father.

Above all, throughout all these years, I have had Ron, the best brother in the world. Just after I moved to Lewes, he started a campaign for my release in the national press, without making any mention of his own. The papers subsequently asked for phone-in votes to test public reaction for or against my release. The public was for me on every occasion.

Sometimes I sit here in my cell with my own thoughts, wondering how and why the Home Office can justify keeping me in prison any longer. I have served a twenty-two-year period of retribution. I also feel that the deterrent argument is no longer applicable, since the murder rate has increased tenfold since 1968. Thirdly, I feel I am no longer a danger to society. I still have all my faculties.

There is also no reason why Ron should not follow me on to the street, because all he needs is a drop of medicine every now and again. Millions of people outside have had a similar breakdown to Ron's all those years ago. We're always reading newspaper stories of slags who commit vicious and unprovoked murders on innocent people. There are hundreds of examples, including one in 1988 when a feller killed someone for no reason, cut the body in 100 pieces and roasted it. He got just six years.

There was one around the same time where a pair of lovers beat a three-year-old girl to death. The doctor who examined her lost count of her bruises after sixty-one. She had a fractured skull and ruptured intestines. The lovers got two years.

Another sickening case involved the gang rape and killing of a fourteen-year-old runaway boy.

We talk about it sometimes on my visits to Ron. I am taken to Broadmoor once every three months or so. We have just recently been allowed to sit together in the main visiting room, after years of being cooped up in a tiny private room, but we are still supervised by two nurses and four prison officers who hear every word of our conversation. I don't know what they think we're going to do. It's a bit ridiculous to suggest we're going to try and escape after twenty-two years.

We have turkey sandwiches and mustard pickle, which is quite a luxury for me.

Ron has a relatively relaxing life in Broadmoor, they treat him OK, and he hasn't been in one bit of trouble since he's been there.

He gets up at 7 am and spends his day reading the newspapers, having conversations with his friends, seeing his visitors when he has them and listening to the radio or tapes on his cassette player. He recently took a liking to the gospel singer, Lon Satton.

Sometimes he does a bit of walking, up and down the shiny, polished passageways. He has a lot of letters to read, and he is very grateful for them, but since his campaign for my release and the accompanying increase in his mail, he finds it impossible to answer all of it.

He has always remembered Alan Lake, Diana Dors's husband, saying, "If you want to grow a beard, grow one," so he does tend to indulge his own impulses, and doesn't really stick to any firm routine. He's locked up again at 9 pm.

He has nothing but good words for Jimmy Savile, who has a high administrative position at Broadmoor. Ron says he has done a lot for the patients because of his modern approach and because he genuinely likes helping people.

It is a hospital for the mentally ill, and one of Ron's favourite stories concerns a conversation he had with another inmate.

This feller was talking about a third patient, and he said, "Of course, you know he's insane . . ."

Ron is surrounded by fascinating characters. There's one chap called Father Joseph, a lovely old man of about sixty-eight. He used to be very violent, but now he's deeply religious. He's not a real priest, but he goes around giving the other patients his blessing. He's been there for years and years.

Ron looks for loyalty and politeness in his friends. He doesn't like arrogant or rude people. One of his favourites is "Gentleman" Danny Clark, a smashing feller with impeccable manners. Ron's known him for over twenty-five years.

Mike Smithers is a man Ron considers to be the bravest in Broadmoor. He attacked a screw, not in the wards but in the punishment block where the screws have everything their own way. He bit a screw's ear half off.

There's another feller called Trevor who's very tall and slim, with big bony hands. He once strangled a man with his bare hands, which is what he's in Broadmoor for. And he massages Ron's neck once a week! He's a very nice feller, apparently. He's always helping the sick people, sitting with them and making tea and coffee, and giving them cigarettes.

One character Ron is not so fond of is a reverend who is known as the "Angel of Death", because they usually only see him when someone is dead. Ron was once asked to be a godfather, and this man of the cloth said he didn't think Ron was a fitting person. Ron said, "Don't speak to me like that, you sanctimonious old bastard!"

In 1987, Ron's first marriage to Elaine started breaking up. She couldn't stand the time he was doing. He had a word and told her it would be better for her if she got a divorce, which she did. They are still very good friends and always will be.

Two years later Ron married again. Kate Howard first wrote to me as a penfriend. Though I cannot keep up a correspondence with all the people who write to me, I chose her letter because it seemed lively, and she had a business letterhead. I'm always interested in any kind of business. We began to exchange letters, and she visited me. I then asked her to visit

Ron, and they fell in love. Some time later, she became Ron's wife.

Of course, there was massive publicity. And there was another burst of publicity even more recently when Ron was named in connection with a vice boy scandal at Broadmoor. That rent boys visited him in privacy at Broadmoor Hospital is totally ridiculous. The security there is tighter than any other establishment in the country. It has bomb-proof walls. Even when I go to visit Ron, we are under strict supervision.

To suggest that he spends time on his own with rent boys is not worth any further comment. It's true to say that anyone can visit Ron if he invites them. Whether or not they look like rent boys is irrelevant. Still, I guess no matter what happens, someone will always be writing something about the Kray twins, whether it's fact or fantasy.

In a way, we are like museum pieces, relics of the past, especially since we are not around the streets to be seen. People still visualize us as we were, physically and mentally. This too creates an enigma type of picture. Is it not right that the more exclusive the club is, the more they want to become members or to see the show? That applies to Ron and me because we are shut away. There was even a hit single about us, Morrissey's *The Last of the Famous International Playboys*, in January 1989. I liked the tune, but I thought the lyrics in their entirety were lacking a little. They came *quite* close . . .

I will listen to anybody and everything on my Murphy. Sometimes when I go to my cell at 8 pm to lock up until the following morning, I turn on the radio just for the sake of hearing another voice. Football commentaries are a favourite of mine, although if Arsenal are playing, I really do take an interest. As I lie in the darkness, after sleeping in a single bed on my own for twenty-one years, I push my feet against the wall and I try to remember what it was like to be in body contact with another person. The warmth of human contact is one thing I do miss.

My reflections in the dark hours are something I feel compelled to express. Perhaps my poem, *Alone At Night*, will convey something of how I feel on my own in my cell.

Alone At Night

Alone at night
  I stay . . .
And it's the same
  Throughout the day,
I've begun to like it
  This way.
I listen to
  my heartbeat
    while most
    are asleep . . .
and enjoy
  my thoughts
of past
  sorrow and joy
    the tears and laughter . . .
all
  in the silence
    of the night . . .
while the stars twinkle bright.
With my deep thoughts
  I toy . . .
of past laughter, sorrow and joy.
To me, silence is golden . . .
  to prayer I am beholden.
Throughout the night
  there's not a stir . . .
    an acorn
      of an idea
        is my spur.
I seek ambitions
  to fulfil . . .
All the time
  the night is still.
I look to a sense
  of fulfilment . . .

177

to an idea
　　that will bring
　　　　agreement.
I am chained
　physically,
　　but my mind
　　　is free.
So I wander
　the night . . .
　　all targets
　　in sight.
My thoughts wander
　beyond the gate . . .
　　as to how
　　　imprisonment
　　　　is
　　　　　my fate.
Is it too much
　that one day
　　I'll be free . . .
It's a day
　that's difficult
　　to foresee.
Especially
　in the aloneness
　　of the night . . .
Such a day seems
　way out of sight.
Yet,
　to dream
　　is my philosophy . . .
　　　that such a day
　　　　I will see.
To me
　each moment
　　is mine . . .
　　　a gem of time

                    I do not wish to see go by.
So there's no rush
   to meet my fate . . .
      even if it means
         beyond the gate.
I try not to fight
   against the tide . . .
      So with each moment
      I ride.
Each day
   is a moment
   of fate . . .
So there's no rush to go
   beyond the gate.
Each day makes me
   free . . .
      because of my
      philosophy.
Is it such a bad fate?

Sometimes, in the dark hours, I mull over my saddest memory of all, the day I was an innocent party to the tragic death of a little boy neighbour when I was just eight years of age. This experience has been etched deeply into my mind and, even today, I feel great sorrow when I think of it.

It happened in Cheshire Street, off Vallance Road. A friend of mine, Alf Miller, used to regularly start up the engine of the Wonderloaf bread van for the driver, and would help to pack the racks. For this, he got a few pence a week. On the day in question, he invited me to come for a ride, and I agreed. He switched on the ignition key and put the gears into action, thinking it was in first gear for forward. But the van shot backwards at great speed. There was a loud crash as it hit an air raid shelter directly behind it. I could hear loud screams. Alf and I rushed round to the back of the van to be confronted with the sight of a little boy with his head smashed in. He was crushed between the van and the air raid shelter. There was blood everywhere. Alf and I ran off in terror, and later on that day the van driver influenced us that we should say nothing at all, and definitely not mention that Alf used to start the van for payment or else he, the van driver, would lose his job. We were eventually called as witnesses at the inquest at the Town Hall, and we gave evidence as the driver had instructed us. The inquest recorded a verdict of accidental death. All these years later, I still despise the van driver who put himself and his retirement pension before everything else. Ironically, the little boy who died was also a twin to a little sister. This was the final, killing detail.

When thinking of the past, and the fact that, thankfully, the good memories override the bad, I recall an old Chinese tale: one day a passer-by came across an old, dilapidated castle. Its thick walls were crumbling and broken, and nearby was a pond which was very still. The passer-by stopped at the edge of the pond and gazed into the stillness of the water which mirrored the old castle. I guess when I sit in my cell and reflect on the past, my thoughts are like that of the passer-by. We tend to remember mostly the great days, and also see some of the ruins and the stillness that are with us today. But we should strive towards the future, regardless of the past. Yesterday is but today's memory, and tomorrow is today's dream. A thousand years have passed by since yesterday.